YOUR recipe could appear in our next cookbook!

Share your tried & true family favorites with us instantly at

www.gooseberrypatch.com

If you'd rather jot 'em down by hand, just mail this form to...

Gooseberry Patch • Cookbooks – Call for Recipes
PO Box 812 • Columbus, OH 43216-0812

If your recipe is selected for a book, you'll receive a FREE copy!

Please share only your original recipes or those that you have made your own over the years.

Recipe Name:

Number of Servings:

Any fond memories about this recipe? Special touches you like to add or handy shortcuts?

Ingredients (include specific measurements):

Instructions (continue on back if needed):

Special Code: **cookbookspage**

Over

Extra space for recipe if needed:

Tell us about yourself...

Your complete contact information is needed so that we can send you your FREE cookbook, if your recipe is published. Phone numbers and email addresses are kept private and will only be used if we have questions about your recipe.

Name:

Address:

City: State: Zip:

Email:

Daytime Phone:

Thank you! Vickie & Jo Ann

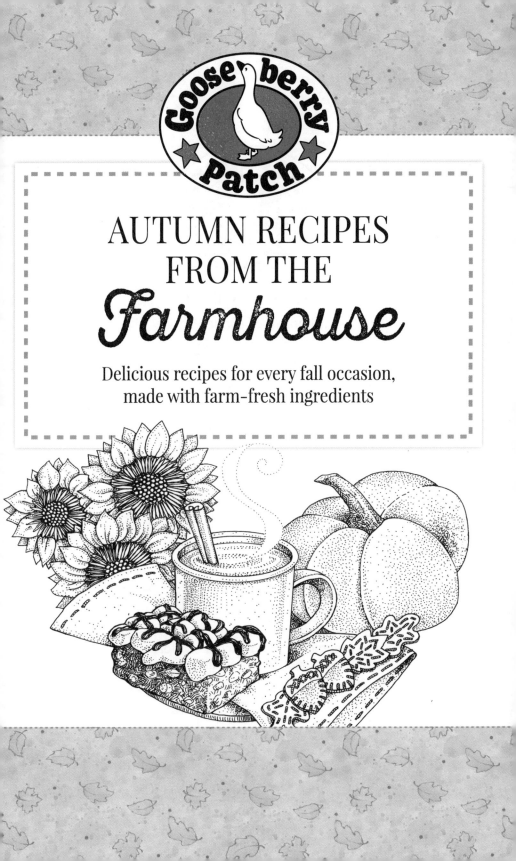

Gooseberry Patch

AUTUMN RECIPES FROM THE
Farmhouse

Delicious recipes for every fall occasion, made with farm-fresh ingredients

Gooseberry Patch

An imprint of Globe Pequot
246 Goose Lane
Guilford, CT 06437

www.gooseberrypatch.com
1•800•854•6673

Copyright 2021, Gooseberry Patch 978-1-62093-437-1

Do you have a tried & true recipe...

tip, craft or memory that you'd like to see featured in a **Gooseberry Patch** cookbook? Visit our website at **www.gooseberrypatch.com** and follow the easy steps to submit your favorite family recipe. Or send them to us at:

Gooseberry Patch
PO Box 812
Columbus, OH 43216-0812

Don't forget to include the number of servings your recipe makes, plus your name, address, phone number and email address. If we select your recipe, your name will appear right along with it... and you'll receive a **FREE** copy of the book!

Contents

Dedication

For everyone who loves all of autumn's pleasures, from the first fallen leaf to the first snowflake, and sharing the best of the harvest with family & friends.

Appreciation

A farm-size thanks to all of you who opened your recipe boxes to share treasured recipes with us.

Favorite Fall Memories

Autumn Recipes
from the Farmhouse

Sweet Farm Memories

Tina Goodpasture
Meadowview, VA

I grew up on a farm on Maiden Creek here in Meadowview, Virginia. We raised chickens, pigs and horses, and grew hay, sugar cane and tobacco. We got our water from a springhouse, where we kept watermelons cold in the summertime. In the evenings, we would have bonfires and roast marshmallows and hot dogs on sticks. Late at night when all was quiet, you could hear the crickets and frogs along the creek. There were no streetlights and it was so dark...you could hear the owls and coyotes too, and I hated to have to go to the outhouse by myself. I was always afraid something was going to get me! Of course, nothing ever did, but it never stopped my brother from trying to scare me! I miss those days. Now I look back and smile at all those times. All my grandparents are gone now. I wish that I could thank them for all the times that we shared on our farm on Maiden Creek.

Favorite Fall Memories

Trick-or-Treating

Cindy Winfield
Nacogdoches, TX

Fifty years ago, I lived in a small neighborhood that had only one road, making a large circle. On Halloween, my mother made her delicious homemade chili. Even though it was one of my favorites, I ate quickly so I could put on my Cinderella costume. The dress was beautiful, but the thin plastic mask made it hard to breathe and sometimes hard to see! I gathered with the other neighborhood kids and away we went from house to house with our pumpkin pails, shouting, "Trick-or-Treat!" Such a fun memory of being with friends and of course, getting all that candy!

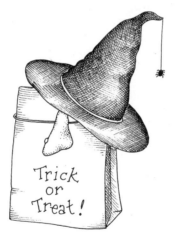

October Birthday Church Dinner

Jill Williams
Riley, KS

I was born in October, and the first Sunday of the month was always the church dinner and bazaar. The day I was born (50 years ago) was the first and nearly the only time my parents have missed that dinner! They still attend, sharing a meal with family, friends and neighbors. Since then, a lot about the day has changed, but not the menu. Nothing says "comfort food" better than homemade chicken & noodles over mashed potatoes and homemade bread!

Autumn Recipes from the Farmhouse

Carving Pumpkins

Charlene McCain
Bakersfield, CA

One of our favorite autumn traditions is carving pumpkins for Halloween. Every year we traveled to the local pumpkin farm to pick out a pumpkin for each of us. Of course, my sons wanted the biggest pumpkins they could find, so we made a rule that you had to be able to carry your own pumpkin. Once we got our pumpkins home, we would scoop out the insides and draw a design or face on the front with a black pen. Carving the pumpkins usually took all afternoon. Once done, we would set them on the front porch, place tea lights inside and wait for it to get dark. The boys loved seeing their designs come to life. My boys are grown now, with families of their own, but they have carried on the tradition of carving pumpkins with their own little ones.

Decorating for Fall

Jennifer Stout
Blandon, PA

I love to decorate for fall. I fill the whole house with fall oranges, yellows and reds. Pumpkins and fall decor are in every room. Candles scented with fall spices and pumpkin scents make me so happy! Then on Halloween, we turn our entire front yard into a cemetery filled with moving ghosts and ghouls. For the past 20 years, we've served 200-plus hot dogs on Halloween to trick-or-treaters. It has become almost a block party in my driveway.

Favorite Fall Memories

High School Football Games

Victoria Vallieres
Greensburg, IN

When I was 16 in 1966, living in central Illinois and a junior in high school, I was dating a football player who was a sophomore. He played junior varsity, so we went to the homecoming game together and sat with a group of friends to cheer on our team, the Purple Raiders. He bought me a huge yellow football mum decorated with a little gold football that I still have in my treasure box. He taught me everything about the game and I became an avid football fan. I still love football and have seen every Super Bowl game from the beginning of the series. This homecoming night, a big yellow harvest moon rose right over the scoreboard as our team won the game! After the game, we walked happily through the rustling leaves to our favorite hangout, Hubbard's Cupboard, to celebrate with burgers and milkshakes. Such good memories!

Autumn Recipes from the Farmhouse

Farm Time with Grandma & Grandpa

Marti Johnston
Circleville, OH

As a young child, I enjoyed nothing more than to spend time with Grandma & Grandpa. My grandparents were busy being farmers, so I spent a lot of time outdoors. I would ride the tractor with Grandpa for hours, loving the smell of the fresh dirt being turned over. If I wasn't with Grandpa, then I was with Grandma. We would work in the garden or spend time getting vegetables ready for canning. I remember spending hours shucking fresh corn so Grandma could can it. But the best memory is of riding with Grandma in the truck to take a supper of cold chicken to Grandpa out in the fields. There was nothing more exciting for me than to drink ice-cold lemonade out of a jar. It is one of the memories I will cherish forever.

Pumpkin Patch

April Bash
Carlisle, PA

There is a church on my children's bus route that has a pumpkin patch for charity every fall. They bring in lots of pumpkins and have a fall fest with a hayride in early October. Ever since they were toddlers, my children have gotten excited when the pumpkins arrive at the church, because they know it's the beginning of cooler weather and then Christmas. Even now, as a middle schooler and a high schooler, they race home from the bus stop to be the first one to tell me that the pumpkins have arrived!

Favorite Fall Memories

Apple Picking

Joan Thamsen
Middletown, NY

Many years ago, a friend and I noticed that her neighbor had an apple tree in his yard. He was an elderly man and she really didn't know him. The apple tree was right by the street, with some of the apples hanging over the curb. Anyway, we saw all the ripe apples and couldn't resist picking them. Well, the man came out, yelling that we were trespassing and stealing his apples. He then told us to never do it again. What did we know? He wasn't picking the apples himself, so we looked at it as helping him out by not letting the apples just fall to the ground and rot. Later that day, I brought the apples home and told my mom what had happened. To make peace with our neighbor, she baked him an apple pie. She made me take it to him and apologize for stealing his apples. When I went back to get the empty pie dish, he told me I could take as many apples as I wanted whenever I wanted as long, as he got one of Mom's apple pies in return. He said it was the best pie he'd ever had!

Autumn Recipes
from the Farmhouse

Special Family Gathering

Judy Loemker
Edwardsville, IL

In fall, a special time comes to mind. On a whim one fall weekend
near Halloween, we decided to build a nice outdoor fire and invite our
three precious little grandchildren and children over. Living on 10 acres,
we quickly gathered firewood and sticks to cut for roasting hot dogs.
The kids were so excited! We had our picnic table loaded with simple
fare...hot dogs and buns, potato chips, baked beans and brownies.
Couldn't forget the marshmallows for toasting after the meal! The little
ones had a great time roasting their "dogs," even though many times
they had more ashes on their hot dogs than nice browned marks. Why
does food always taste so delicious outside? After toasting the last of
the marshmallows, we spread blankets in the field nearby to relax in
the sun and enjoy the beautiful weather. "Pee Paw" had other ideas,
however! He had just found a rubber "bloody hand" at the local
Walmart and was determined to use it that day. He would sneak up on
the girls and place that ugly hand near them as they screamed their
heads off. He chased them around in the field with it as they quickly ran
to escape its ugliness. They laughed and laughed! Every once in awhile,
they would take it away from him and the tables would be turned. I
have some amazing pictures of that day to treasure! Everyone had a
great time, the food was easy, and we finally got the marshmallow goo
off of everyone. The kids still remember that day and all the fun we
had too. I think we'll have to try this again, now that we have seven
grandbabies to love. Well worth the simple efforts!

Favorite Fall Memories

Literary Lunches

Dale-Harriet Rogovich
Madison, WI

For a few weeks in the early 1950s when I was in elementary school, my mother had a job outside the house, so I had lunch every day with my schoolmate and neighbor, Davey. His mom read to us while we ate lunch, and the first day or two of a new storybook always "matched" the book. For lunch the first day of *Heidi*, we had thick slices of buttered warm fresh bread with slabs of cheese and milk to drink out of bowls, just like Heidi did! On the first day of *Robinson Crusoe*, Davey's mother had cut big green tropical leaves out of green construction paper. She made skewers with cubes of glazed ham, pineapple, green pepper and maraschino cherries and gave us pineapple juice to drink. We both looked forward to hearing the stories, and I've always remembered the special first day of each story.

Mom's Homemade Halloween Treats

Kathi Yoswick
Aliquippa, PA

This time of year, I always think back to my mom making us homemade doughnuts for Halloween. In our neighborhood, each mom had a fall specialty that she would make for Halloween. After us kids returned from trick-or-treating, we would meet at one of the homes and get to sample all the goodies. We had everything from candy apples and fudge, to stuffed peanut butter cookies, hot apple cider and the best of all, my mom's homemade doughnuts. It all made for some delicious memories!

Autumn Recipes from the Farmhouse

Building a Leaf Palace

Debra Padden
Andover, NY

My sister and I grew up in a small village in western New York, full of tree lined streets that turned all shades of orange, red and yellow every fall. Our dad was a self-employed building contractor and one fall day, we decided to be like him and build a leaf house! Did you ever build one? They look like a house blueprint, with lines and spaces indicating the bedrooms, closets, doors and windows! We gathered all the neighborhood kids and soon realized that to accomplish such a grand-scale project, we needed many more leaves! Kids ran home and soon came back with bags, baskets and wagons full of leaves from all over town! We raked and raked and built our mansion. It was the envy of all who saw it...even the other parents who came to admire! They all seemed so happy! All except for our dad. His expression as he pulled his truck into the driveway was not the one we expected at all! We thought turning our yard, that had been mostly clear of beautiful leaves, into a leaf palace was a fine idea!

Favorite Fall Memories

Snapping Beans with Nannie
Dawn Bastounes
Grant, MI

Now that the farmers' markets are running here in Michigan, I am reminded of all the time spent in my Nannie's garden in Harford County, Maryland. As a matter of fact, today I'm cooking green beans, ham, and taters just like Nannie taught me. When I was little, I learned to snap beans and shell peas on her back porch. Before we arrived, she would go to the garden and fill paper bags with beans or peas. Then, we would sit on the back porch to snap and shell them. When they were cooked up, they smelled so good! They tasted even better, cooked with all the love she had, and with cornbread on the side. Years ago, I had the pleasure of teaching my older children to snap beans, side by side with me. I love you, Nannie!

Goofy Girls!
Toni Leathers
Claremont, CA

When I was growing up, we lived in Connecticut and had gorgeous fall weather, and a bazillion leaves in our yard. My sisters and I had the job of raking all those leaves. My favorite jacket was one with a leaf pattern on it, of course! I used to think that when I wore the jacket, I could hide in the piles and they wouldn't be able to see me, then I would jump up and try to scare them! I'm sure they were hip to my prank, but went along with it anyway! Those were the carefree days...I wish I could go back to them!

𝒜utumn Recipes from the 𝒥armhouse

Harvesting Sugar Cane

Tammy Johnson
Seguin, TX

Among my fondest memories of growing up in Missouri are the memories of making molasses. My grandfather grew his own sugarcane, and each fall the entire family and many friends gathered to help with the whole process. We'd harvest the sugarcane and pile it on flatbed trailers. The teenagers and older children, wielding knives, would cut the heads from all the stalks of cane. Grandpa would push the cane through a press to squeeze its juices. Everyone helped stir the cooking molasses in huge pans over roaring fires. The handles of our stirrers were the length of broomsticks! The very best part of the process was after the pans had been poured into jars. We all took fresh homemade biscuits or the ends of sugarcane and scraped the remaining molasses from the bottoms of the pans to sample and eat. Yum! The smell was simply divine.

Favorite Fall Memories

Raking and Riding

Mary Simpson
Brick, NJ

I remember when my brothers and I were little, we would "help" Dad rake the backyard leaves by filling our wheelbarrow with armloads of leaves from the piles he raked. He would then pile the three of us on top of the filled barrow and wheel us to the front curb, where he would dump the entire contents onto the other leaves he'd raked into the street. We kids were laughing and screaming all the way. When the raking was done, Dad would let us sit on the front steps of the house to watch the leaf bonfire burn as he stood by with the hose, ready to douse the ashes. Those wonderful memories still hold strong for me, and are just one of the reasons autumn is my favorite season!

Arkansas Autumn Memories

Beckie Apple
Grannis, AR

I grew up in the small rural country community of Blue Ball, Arkansas. I looked forward to the autumn activities that we experienced on the farm. Ours was a working farm family life. We had cows, pigs, chickens and a horse or two. Autumn was a time for finishing up our large vegetable garden and getting ready for cold winters. As a young girl, I remember the first sign of autumn was the beautiful colored leaves that fell. The oak trees dropped their acorns and covered the ground around our house. The first nips of cold morning air reminded me of what was to come, when a jacket would be necessary for playing outside. I loved the sweet smell of burning leaves and the smoke from chimney fires in our small community. It was a cherished memory of my mom and grandmothers' kitchens that seemed to always have a wonderful aroma of baked bread and apple pies.

Autumn Recipes from the Farmhouse

Campfire Soup & Sandwiches
Caroline Timbs
Cord, AR

A favorite memory of mine happened a few years ago, when we had a fire pit dinner at a neighbor's farm. It was a soup & sandwiches dinner. Potato soup was cooked in an iron pot hung over the fire. This potato soup was farm-fresh, made with farm-grown potatoes, farm-fresh chicken broth and ham from a local hog farmer. This was the first time I had ever tasted potato soup...it was so delicious! I don't know if it was the fresh ingredients or the iron pot, but I have never forgotten about that soup. The sandwiches were a new idea for our family as well. I was in charge of bringing the grilled cheese supplies to cook over the fire, which we'd never done before. These sandwiches tasted smoked, like something you would get from a high-end barbecue joint. I loved them...we all enjoyed them! I can't wait to get another chance to cook grilled cheese over another fire pit. You never know what new ideas you will learn from those around you.

Favorite Fall Memories

Halloween Memories

Melissa Flasck
Rochester Hills, Mi

One of the best parts of autumn is Halloween. In my family, we would always go trick-or-treating around our neighborhood. The Jack-o'-Lanterns were always burning brightly on everyone's porches. Then we would drive to my grandparents' house to show off our costumes and visit with them. Grandma always passed out the best jumbo-size candy bars! As a parent now, I continue this tradition with my own children and their grandparents.

Autumn on the Farm

Kelli Wells
Coal City, IN

My husband and I live on his grandparents' Black Angus cattle farm here in Indiana. Autumn is the time of year to prepare for the long winter days, after the crops are in and the hay is done. On the day when my husband and son winterize and store the farm equipment, my daughter and I spend some time together in our 130-year-old farmhouse kitchen, preparing a cozy meal of soup and dessert for the four of us to share. What a lovely way to end the cool autumn days, reminiscing about the old days on the farm!

Autumn Recipes from the Farmhouse

Roasting Pumpkin Seeds

Constance Bockstoce
Dallas, GA

My favorite fall memory always came after we'd cut a pumpkin into a Jack-o'-Lantern. My mother would take the seeds and pull off most of the membrane, leaving tiny bits attached to the seeds. Then she would lightly oil a cookie sheet and spread the seeds in the thinnest layer possible. Then she would lightly salt the seeds before putting them in the oven at 350 degrees. While waiting for them to bake golden brown, we would drink hot cocoa with marshmallows and talk about what we were going to wear for trick-or-treating. When the seeds were done, we snacked on them until we were full. Rarely were there any left! I have done this with my children and my grandchildren and the home-baked pumpkin seeds are still my favorite.

The Smell of Autumn

Terri McCauley
Antelope, MT

I remember when I was about seven years old, I couldn't wait for autumn to come. It meant playing in the leaves and smelling the autumn air...it was crisp and so clean! We lived in Connecticut then, and the apples had to be picked into a bushel basket. Our neighbor had a pear tree and we always traded apples and pears! Then my Mom would bake with the apples, or we would eat as many as she would allow us to have without getting a bellyache! I'm happy to have these wonderful memories.

Favorite Fall Memories

The Golden Rake

Patricia Jones
Newton, NJ

I grew up in a family of six children. This is great when you have a big yard full of fallen leaves...many hands makes less work! I had four brothers and one much younger sister. All except Baby Sis were deployed in the leaf-raking effort. Everyone had a rake. My very clever dad spray-painted my rake gold! Being the princess that I was, I happily skipped out of the garage with my golden rake in hand to join the boys cleaning up the leaves! It still makes me smile to recall this memory.

Pumpkin Patch Memories

Cindy Slawski
Medford Lakes, NJ

Though my mother has been gone for many years, I always think of her when the leaves start changing and the air gets cooler. As a child, every year when October rolled around, we would go to our local pumpkin patch and search for the perfect pumpkin. Once we found "the right one" we would go home, heat up some cider and carve a Jack-o'-Lantern for the front porch. My mom always made chocolate chip cookies for the occasion. Sometimes when October arrives again, I can still smell those cookies.

Autumn Recipes from the Farmhouse

October Chili Memories

Glenda Reynolds
Millersport, OH

Every October for the last 35 years at least, our entire family has gathered at our little mini-farm, the Reynolds Homestead, for a fall Halloween gathering. It is a time of fun and good food. The barn is set up with long tables loaded with food offerings such as homemade chips and salsas, desserts and a Halloweeny punch to accompany Paw's famous chili, lovingly called "October Chili." October Chili starts early on the day of the gathering, in a big cast-iron Dutch oven over an open fire in our fire pit. Paw would begin by browning his mixture of beef, pork and onions. Over the morning, he added all the other special ingredients, and he cooked it all day outside over the open fire. It was eagerly anticipated, and each year our family declared it the best chili ever! (If you'd like to try it yourself, you'll find the recipe on page 66.) Although Paw has passed on these 8 years ago, we continue to make October Chili, emphasizing that his children and grandchildren continue the tradition. We enjoy the delicious chili with hot dogs roasted over the open fire for a complete meal. The evening is topped off with apple dumplings, cookies and all things Halloween. Then we read Halloween-themed stories, sing songs and trick-or-treat around the campfire. We all go on a haunted hayride and a good time is had by all. What fond memories and wonderful continued family traditions!

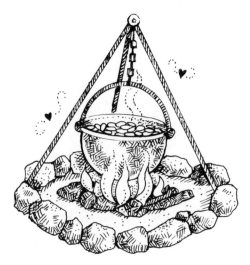

Favorite Fall Memories

Cozy Fall Bonfire

Bree Phoebe
Holland, TX

When I was a child, every fall when the nights would get longer, we would have a neighborly bonfire on our little country road. Anything that could be roasted on a stick, from sausage to corn on the cob, was put over the fire. Hot punch or tea was served, and the best part was apples sprinkled in cinnamon and wrapped in foil put near the fire to bake...yum! It's been years since I've been to one of these get-togethers, but it is such a fun memory.

Autumn Birthdays

Elaine Divis
Sioux City, IA

Autumn is my favorite season by far! Those warm sunny days and cool crisp evenings are just two reasons. High school football games and watching the band perform at halftime, bonfires and weenie roasts, chili and cinnamon rolls at suppertime are all memorable. But the very best reasons to love fall are the birthdays of my second grandson Howie, who shares my September birthday, and my oldest grandson Henry on Halloween!

Autumn Recipes from the Farmhouse

Apple Butter Stirrin'

Diane Watson
Newark, OH

My favorite harvest memory is of my grandma and the yearly apple butter stirrin' she hosted at her farm in Heath, Ohio. It became a reunion of sorts, with lots of family & friends gathering for the full day event. It would start the night before with the peeling of the apples...
16 bushels of them! Then, very early in the morning, my grandpa started the fire and hung up the large 40-gallon copper kettle that we would cook the apples in. Everyone would bring covered dishes and make a day out of it. It was so much fun smelling the wood burning and stirring with the large wooden paddles. The best part was getting to eat the freshly made apple butter on the homemade breads and rolls that everyone brought!

The Pumpkin Patch

Laura Fredlund
Papillion, NE

I have a peculiar love for pumpkins. I can't compare my love for pumpkins to anything, just that they bring me joy. My family and I are fortunate to live near an amazing pumpkin patch that has fun activities, and beautiful scenery that many people gather to see each fall. Imagine the perfect autumn scenery, crunchy, colorful leaves, cornstalks, cooler temperatures and the smells of kettle corn and wood smoke in the air. It's a glorious feeling leaving the heat of summer and stepping into the beauty of autumn. I love visiting the playful and fun "haunted house." Taking a hayride to the pumpkin patch for the first time, where thousands and thousands of pumpkins spread across the fields like an ocean of orange, is one of my absolute favorite memories. Perhaps one of the most romantic things my husband has said to me is "I'll get you any pumpkin you want, dear!"

24

Oh, What
a Beautiful
Morning!

Autumn Recipes from the Farmhouse

Farmers' Breakfast Casserole

Ed & Judy Phelan
Macomb, IL

We have been making and enjoying this delicious breakfast recipe since the early 1990s.

8 eggs, lightly beaten
1 c. milk
1/4 t. pepper
Optional: 1/2 t. salt,
   1 t. dry mustard
6 slices bread, cut into
   small cubes

1/2 lb. ground pork sausage,
   browned and drained
1/2 lb. baked ham, finely
   chopped
1 to 1-1/2 c. shredded sharp
   Cheddar cheese

In a large bowl, whisk together eggs, milk and seasonings. Add remaining ingredients; mix well. Transfer mixture to a buttered 13"x9" baking pan. Cover and refrigerate overnight. Uncover; bake at 350 degrees for 45 minutes, or until bubbly and eggs are set. Serves 6 to 8.

On weekend mornings in autumn, take time to enjoy a hearty family breakfast...warm biscuits with homemade jam, flapjacks with maple syrup, crisp bacon, sausage and farm-fresh eggs!

Oh, What a Beautiful Morning!

Early Morning Eggs

Caroline Timbs
Cord, AR

This recipe is perfect for using up leftover pan-fried or roasted potatoes. Tasty with a side of maple sausage...very easy to halve for fewer servings!

2 T. butter
1 onion, chopped
2 green peppers, chopped
8-oz. pkg. sliced mushrooms

2 c. cooked potatoes, diced
1 doz. eggs, beaten
1/2 c. shredded Cheddar cheese

Melt butter in a large skillet over medium heat. Add onion, peppers and mushrooms; sauté until tender. Add potatoes; heat through. Reduce heat to medium-low; pour in eggs. Cook, stirring often, until set. Top with cheese; cover and let stand until melted. Makes 8 to 10 servings.

Momma Lou's Apple–Apple Oatmeal

Lisa Wood
Princeton, MN

I came up with this recipe one fall day when we had fresh apple cider from a farm...with three little boys, it's a staple at our house. Apple juice can be substituted for the cider and it's just as good.

1-3/4 c. apple cider
1 apple, peeled, cored and
  shredded
1 c. old-fashioned oats,
  uncooked

Garnish: light cream, brown
  sugar

Combine cider and apple in a saucepan; bring to a boil over medium heat. Stir in oats. Cook for 5 minutes, stirring often, or until thickened. Top with cream and brown sugar. Serves 2.

Treat yourself to an old farmhouse tradition...a big slice of apple or cherry pie for breakfast!

Blueberry Oatmeal Muffins

Elisha Nelson
Brookline, MO

These delicious muffins remind me of my dad. He passed away a few years ago, but I am reminded of him every time I pull out this recipe card written in his handwriting!

1 c. buttermilk
1 c. quick-cooking oats,
    uncooked
3/4 c. brown sugar, packed
1 egg, beaten
1/4 c. butter, melted
1 T. vanilla extract
1 T. baking powder

1/2 t. baking soda
1/2 t. salt
1/2 t. nutmeg
1 t. cinnamon
1 c. all-purpose or whole-wheat
    flour
1/2 c. chopped pecans or walnuts
1-1/3 c. fresh blueberries

In a small bowl, combine buttermilk and oats; set aside. In a large bowl, combine brown sugar, egg, butter, vanilla, baking powder, baking soda, salt and spices. Stir in oat mixture. Add flour, stirring just until combined. Fold in nuts and blueberries. Spoon batter into 12 greased muffin cups, filling 3/4 full. Bake at 400 degrees for 15 to 20 minutes. Makes one dozen.

Make a simple fabric liner for a basket of fresh-baked muffins. Use pinking shears to cut an 18-inch square of cotton fabric in a sweet fall print. So easy...why not make one for the breakfast table and an extra for gift-giving?

Oh, What a Beautiful Morning!

Apple Ring Fritters

Bobbi Crosson
Toledo, OH

My three sons loved these fritters with sausages. I didn't always get any, as they ate them as fast as I could make them! Oil may be used in place of shortening. Good for breakfast or supper.

2 c. all-purpose flour
1-1/2 c. milk
3 T. sugar
1 T. baking powder
1/2 t. salt
2 eggs, beaten

shortening for deep frying
6 to 8 apples, peeled, cored and
    cut into thin rings
Garnish: warm maple syrup or
    powdered sugar

In a large bowl, combine flour, milk, sugar, baking powder, salt and eggs. Stir to make a batter; set aside. In an electric or stovetop skillet over medium heat, melt 2 to 3 inches shortening. Working in batches, dip apple rings into batter. Add to hot shortening, a few at a time, and cook, turning after lightly golden on one side. Drain on paper towels. Serve warm, garnished as desired. Serves 3 to 4.

Cook up some country-style sausage patties. To one pound ground pork, add one teaspoon ground sage, 3/4 teaspoon salt, 3/4 teaspoon pepper and 1/4 teaspoon brown sugar. Blend well, form into patties and fry in a skillet...delicious!

Autumn Recipes from the Farmhouse

Easy Sticky Pecan Rolls

Elizabeth Smithson
Mayfield, KY

This is a shortcut I've found to Granny's yummy sweet rolls. Just as good and doesn't take so long!

1 c. chopped pecans, divided
12 frozen yeast rolls
3-1/2 oz. pkg. cook & serve
   butterscotch pudding mix

1/2 c. butter
1/2 c. brown sugar, packed
cinnamon to taste

Sprinkle 1/2 cup nuts in a greased Bundt® pan or 13"x9" baking pan. Arrange frozen rolls on top of nuts; sprinkle with dry pudding and set aside. In a small saucepan, combine butter and brown sugar. Bring to a boil over medium heat, stirring until sugar dissolves. Spoon over rolls. Cover with greased aluminum foil; let rise overnight at room temperature. In the morning, uncover; sprinkle with remaining nuts and cinnamon. Bake at 350 degrees for 30 minutes. Immediately turn rolls out of pan; serve warm. Makes one dozen.

Simple farmhouse-style table decorations are often the most charming! Fill a rustic wooden bowl with shiny red apples or scented pine cones for the kitchen table.

Oh, What a Beautiful Morning!

Country-Style Egg Skillet

Liz Blackstone
Racine, WI

I never have to call "Come & get it!" when this yummy dish is on the stove. My family comes running at the first scent of frying bacon! Leftover cooked redskins are fine...just heat through.

8 slices bacon, chopped	8 eggs, beaten
2 c. redskin potatoes, diced	1/4 c. milk
salt and pepper to taste	1 t. salt
1/2 c. onion, diced	1/4 t. pepper
1/2 c. red or green pepper, diced	1 c. shredded Cheddar cheese

In a large skillet over medium heat, cook bacon until crisp. Remove bacon to paper towels, reserving drippings in skillet. Add potatoes to drippings; cook over medium heat until tender and golden, about 10 to 12 minutes. Season potatoes with salt and pepper. Add onion and green pepper; cook and stir for 3 to 4 minutes, until crisp-tender. Drain; stir in bacon. In a large bowl, whisk together eggs, milk, salt and pepper; pour over vegetables in skillet. Cook and stir until eggs are set as desired. Sprinkle with cheese; let stand until melted. Serves 4.

Save bacon drippings in a jar kept in the fridge. For delicious farm-style flavor, add just a spoonful to the oil when frying potatoes.

Autumn Recipes
from the Farmhouse

Pumpkin Spice Pancakes

Brenda Lenz
Georgetown, TX

Pumpkin pancakes are one of my favorite ways to celebrate fall! I have searched far and wide for a good recipe and I think I may have finally come up with it. They're sweet, but not too sweet, and they have a definite pumpkiny-ness. This batter is thick, so spread it out a bit when you drop it onto the griddle. Don't be tempted to thin it out... it's part of what makes these pancakes light and fluffy. Serve with warm maple syrup for a true taste of fall!

1-1/2 c. fat-free evaporated milk
1 c. canned pumpkin
1 egg, beaten
2 T. oil
2 T. cider vinegar
2 c. whole-wheat pastry flour
1/4 c. brown sugar, packed

2 t. baking powder
1 t. baking soda
1 t. pumpkin pie spice
1 t. cinnamon
1/2 t. salt
Optional: semi-sweet chocolate
   chips

In a bowl, stir together evaporated milk, pumpkin, egg, oil and vinegar; set aside. In a separate bowl, combine flour, brown sugar, baking powder, baking soda, spices and salt. Stir flour mixture into pumpkin mixture, just enough to combine. Heat a lightly oiled griddle or skillet over medium-high heat. Pour or scoop batter onto hot griddle, using 1/3 cup for each pancake. If desired, drop a few chocolate chips onto each pancake. Brown on both sides and serve hot. Serves 6 to 8.

Spice up an autumn breakfast with some cider-glazed sausages. Brown and drain 1/2 pound breakfast sausage links. Pour a cup of apple cider into the skillet, turn the heat down to low and simmer for 10 minutes. Yummy!

Oh, What a Beautiful Morning!

Sausage Biscuits

Marcia Shaffer
Conneaut Lake, PA

A very old recipe from my family. It's scrumptious...no wonder the recipe has been kept for generations!

1 lb. ground country pork
   sausage
3/4 c. butter, softened
1-1/2 c. shredded extra sharp
   Cheddar cheese
1/4 c. shredded Parmesan cheese

1-1/2 c. plus 2 T. all-purpose
   flour
1 t. salt
1/2 t. pepper
Optional: pecan halves

Brown sausage in a skillet over medium heat; drain and set aside. In a large bowl, blend butter and cheeses; set aside. In a separate bowl, mix flour, salt and pepper. Add flour mixture to butter mixture; blend together using a wooden spoon. Crumble sausage; add to dough and mix in with your hands. Cover and chill dough 30 minutes. Pinch off small pieces of dough and roll into one-inch balls. Arrange balls on ungreased baking sheets, one inch apart. If desired, top each ball with a pecan half, flattening the balls. Bake at 350 degrees for 15 to 20 minutes. Serve warm or at room temperature. Refrigerate in an airtight container up to one week, or freeze. Makes about 6 dozen.

On Thanksgiving morning, serve fuss-free favorites like Sausage Biscuits...ideal for overnight guests. Everyone can easily help themselves while the day's fun is beginning.

Amy's Awesome Sausage Ring

Amy Thomason Hunt
Traphill, NC

This is a must-have at Thanksgiving, Christmas and gal-time gatherings. For a great brunch dish, spoon scrambled eggs into the center of the ring after it's baked and onto a serving platter.

1 lb. ground pork breakfast
   sausage
1 green pepper, finely diced
3/4 c. onion, finely diced
1 lb. frozen bread dough, thawed
grated Parmesan cheese and
   garlic salt to taste

8-oz. pkg. shredded mozzarella
   cheese
Garnish: warm pizza sauce or
   sausage gravy for dipping

Brown sausage in a skillet over medium heat, adding pepper and onion during the last few minutes of cooking; drain. Meanwhile, on a lightly floured surface, spread dough into a 15-inch by 10-inch rectangle. Sprinkle dough with Parmesan cheese and garlic salt. Spoon sausage mixture onto dough; spread mixture to within one inch of edges of dough. Top with mozzarella cheese. Roll up, starting on one long edge; form into a ring. Place dough ring in a Bundt® pan sprayed with non-stick vegetable spray; pinch the ends together. Top with additional Parmesan cheese. Bake at 350 degrees for 20 to 25 minutes, until golden. Turn out onto a serving platter; serve with desired dipping sauce. Serves 8 to 10.

Tuck a bunch of fresh flowers
into a Mason jar to add a special
touch to breakfast...no flower
arranging skills needed!

Oh, What a Beautiful Morning!

Cranberry Puffs

Molly Ebert
Columbus, IN

*If it's fall, it's time to make the cranberry puffs! I love
serving them to family & friends for brunch.*

1 c. cranberry-orange relish,
  divided
1 c. biscuit baking mix

1/4 c. sugar
1 egg, beaten
1/3 c. milk

Into each of 8 greased muffin cups, spoon 2 tablespoons cranberry-orange relish; set aside. Mix together remaining ingredients in a bowl; spoon into muffin cups, filling 2/3 full. Bake at 400 degrees for 15 minutes, or until tops are golden. Invert puffs onto a wire rack to cool. Serve warm, topped with Butter Sauce. Serves 8.

Butter Sauce:

1/2 c. sugar
1/4 c. light cream

1/4 c. butter, sliced
1/2 t. vanilla extract

In a small saucepan, combine sugar and cream. Bring to a boil over medium heat, stirring constantly. Remove from heat; whisk in butter and vanilla.

A weekend morning is the perfect time for getting together to chat over coffee cake and coffee. Invite a girlfriend, or the new neighbor you've been wanting to get to know better, to share the latest news. You'll be so glad you did!

Autumn Recipes from the Farmhouse

Simple French Toast

Vickie
Gooseberry Patch

Just an old-fashioned way to make something delicious from a few eggs, a little milk and some bread. Mom always said that day-old bread actually works better than fresh. Enjoy!

3 eggs, beaten
2/3 c. half-and-half or
   whole milk
2 T. sugar or pure maple syrup
1 t. vanilla extract
1/4 t. salt

3 T. butter, divided
6 slices white or egg bread,
   crusts trimmed if desired
Garnish: powdered sugar, butter,
   maple syrup

In a shallow bowl, whisk together eggs, half-and-half or milk, sugar or syrup, vanilla and salt; set aside. Melt 2 tablespoons butter in a skillet over medium heat. Dip 2 slices bread into egg mixture on both sides until saturated. Transfer to skillet and cook until golden on both sides. Repeat with remaining egg mixture, bread and butter. Dust slices with powdered sugar; serve with butter and syrup. Makes 6 servings.

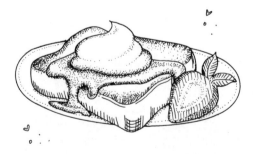

Whip up a luscious topping to dollop on waffles and French toast...
yum! Combine 3/4 cup whipping cream, 2 tablespoons softened
cream cheese and one tablespoon powdered sugar. Beat with an
electric mixer on medium speed until soft peaks form. Keep
refrigerated in a small covered crock.

Oh, What a Beautiful Morning!

Scrambled Eggs Supreme

Janis Parr
Ontario, Canada

This simple recipe makes the best scrambled eggs!
Serve piping hot over hot buttered toast.

8 eggs, beaten
1-1/2 T. mayonnaise
1-1/2 T. all-purpose flour
1 t. onion, finely minced
salt and pepper to taste
1 T. butter

In a bowl, whisk eggs, mayonnaise and flour until smooth. Stir in onion and seasonings; set aside. Melt butter in a skillet over medium heat; add egg mixture. Cook, stirring constantly, until eggs are cooked as desired. Makes 4 servings.

Country-Style Breakfast Potatoes

Kelly Alderson
Erie, PA

My family can't get enough of these hearty potatoes! Sometimes
I'll add some chopped onion to the potatoes.

1-1/2 lbs. redskin potatoes, cubed
5 slices bacon
3/4 c. cooked ham, diced
1 c. shredded Cheddar cheese
1/2 t. seasoned salt
1/4 t. pepper
Optional: sour cream, chopped fresh chives

Cover potatoes with water in a microwave-safe dish. Cover with plastic wrap. Microwave on high for 4 to 5 minutes, until fork-tender; drain. Meanwhile, in a large skillet over medium heat, cook bacon until crisp. Remove bacon to paper towels; reserve drippings in skillet. Add potatoes to drippings; sauté until golden. Add crumbled bacon, ham, cheese and seasonings. Cook and stir over medium heat until cheese is melted. Garnish as desired. Serves 6.

All seasons sweet, but autumn best of all.

–Elinor Wylie

Autumn Recipes from the Farmhouse

Maple-Pumpkin Walnut Oatmeal Bake

Courtney Stultz
Weir, KS

If you're looking for a delicious fall or winter breakfast, this is a good recipe! It is hearty and filling, plus you can make it the night before and bake the next morning. Great for holiday breakfasts!

1 c. canned pumpkin
1 c. milk
2 eggs, beaten
1/2 c. pure maple syrup
1/2 c. brown sugar, packed
1 t. vanilla extract
1 T. cinnamon

1 t. ground cardamom
2 t. baking soda
1/2 t. salt
3 c. old-fashioned oats, uncooked
1/2 c. chopped walnuts
Optional: additional 1 c. milk

In a large bowl, mix together pumpkin, milk, eggs, maple syrup, brown sugar, vanilla, spices, baking soda and salt. Stir in oats and walnuts until combined. Spoon into a greased 3-quart casserole dish. Bake, uncovered, at 350 degrees for about 30 minutes, until set. For a make-ahead option, cover and refrigerate overnight. In the morning, uncover, pour one cup additional milk over the top, if desired; bake as directed. Makes 10 servings.

Pure maple syrup is labeled with various names according to strength. Golden is very delicate, perfect for candy making. Amber has a rich taste you'll love on pancakes and waffles. Dark and Very Dark indicates a robust flavor that's just right in baking and in glazes. They're all delicious!

Oh, What a Beautiful Morning!

Mom's Cranberry Tea

Heather Bartlett
Marietta, GA

It wouldn't be Thanksgiving Day without this special tea! When I was a child, my mom always made it and she still does. I've continued this tradition in my own home. You may wish to enclose the whole spices in a muslin bag for convenience.

4 qts. water, divided
3 4-inch cinnamon sticks
30 whole cloves
15-oz. can jellied cranberry sauce

12-oz. can frozen orange juice
    concentrate, thawed
1 c. sugar
6 T. lemon juice

In a small saucepan over medium heat, combine 2 cups water, cinnamon sticks and cloves. Bring to a boil; boil for 10 minutes. Meanwhile, in a large saucepan, stir together cranberry sauce, orange juice, sugar and lemon juice. Strain boiling spice liquid into cranberry sauce mixture; discard spices. Add remaining water. Heat through over medium-low heat, stirring occasionally. Serve hot. Makes about 5 quarts.

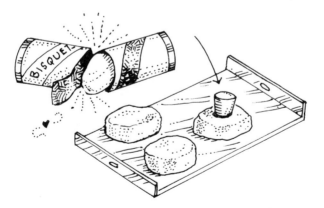

Doughnuts in a dash! Separate refrigerated biscuits and cut a hole in the center of each with a thimble. Fry biscuits in hot oil until golden on both sides; drain on paper towels. Roll in sugar and serve warm.

Autumn Recipes from the Farmhouse

Hearty Sausage & Rice Bake

Shirley Howie
Foxboro, MA

This delicious creamy, savory casserole is one of my favorites!
It is perfect for brunch, lunch, dinner or even as a side dish
for a Thanksgiving or Christmas meal.

1 lb. ground pork sausage
8-oz. pkg. sliced mushrooms
2 stalks celery, coarsely chopped
1 red pepper, coarsely chopped
1 onion, coarsely chopped
1 t. dried thyme
1/2 t. dried oregano

6-oz. pkg. long-grain and wild
   rice mix, divided
1-3/4 c. chicken broth
10-3/4 oz. can cream of
   mushroom soup
1 c. shredded Cheddar cheese,
   divided

In a skillet over medium-high heat, cook sausage until well browned, stirring often to separate. Drain. Add mushrooms, celery, red pepper, onion, seasonings and rice seasoning packet to skillet. Cook until vegetables are tender-crisp. Spoon mixture into a greased 13"x9" baking pan. Add rice mix, chicken broth, soup and 1/2 cup cheese; stir until well combined. Cover and bake at 375 degrees for one hour, or until rice is tender. At serving time, stir; sprinkle with remaining cheese. Makes 6 servings.

Mix up a fresh poppy seed dressing for fruit salad. Combine
1/4 cup oil, 3 tablespoons honey, 2 tablespoons lemon juice and
1-1/2 teaspoons poppy seed. Drizzle over your favorite fruits...
it's scrumptious with cubed oranges, pineapple, apples and grapes.

Oh, What a Beautiful Morning!

Sunburst Muffins

Jolene Finnie
Ontario, Canada

*This is a great, fast and easy recipe. The muffins freeze well,
if you want to make them ahead of time.*

2 c. all-purpose flour
1/2 c. brown sugar, packed
2 t. baking soda
1/2 t. salt
15-oz. can fruit cocktail

1 tart apple, cored and grated
3 eggs, beaten
2/3 c. oil
2 t. vanilla extract

In a large bowl, mix together flour, brown sugar, baking soda and salt.
Add fruit cocktail with juice and remaining ingredients; stir until
moistened. Spoon batter into 12 to 14 lightly greased muffin cups,
filling 2/3 full. Bake at 350 degrees for 25 minutes. Makes 12 to
14 muffins.

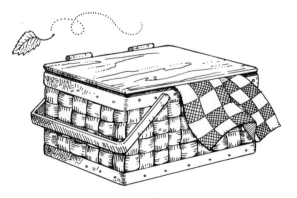

After a hearty breakfast, pack a picnic lunch and hop in the car.
Take a favorite route to see the fall color, or go down that country
lane you've always wondered about...who knows where it will lead?

Autumn Recipes from the Farmhouse

Apple Butter Cinnamon Rolls
Laura Witham
Anchorage, AK

I love the holidays, and my absolute favorite part about them is waking up early and making breakfast for my family. After making cinnamon rolls that were dry and not awesome at all, I decided to try adding apple butter to the centers of the rolls. It did the trick...now my family can't get enough of them!

3/4 c. warm water, 110 to
   115 degrees
2 envs. active dry yeast
1/2 c. sugar
1 t. salt
2 eggs, beaten
1/2 c. shortening
1/2 c. butter

4 c. all-purpose flour
1 T. cinnamon
3/4 c. apple butter
1/2 c. brown sugar, packed
Garnish: additional cinnamon,
   16-oz. container cream
   cheese icing

In a large bowl, combine all ingredients except apple butter, brown sugar and garnish; mix until well blended. Knead for 10 minutes, or until dough is well formed. (If using a bread maker, set to dough setting; combine ingredients as above and process according to manufacturer's directions. Continue as directed.) Place dough in a greased large bowl. Cover and let rise until double, 45 to 60 minutes; punch down. Remove dough to a floured surface. With a rolling pin, roll dough into a rectangle, about 1/4-inch thick. Spread apple butter evenly over dough; crumble brown sugar over it. Sprinkle generously with cinnamon to taste. Starting on one long edge, roll up dough jelly-roll style. Slice into 8 rounds; arrange in a well-greased 11"x7" baking pan. Bake at 350 degrees for 15 to 20 minutes, until golden. While still hot, spread with frosting. Makes 8 rolls.

When baking with yeast, if the water added to yeast is too hot, it will kill the yeast. Try Grandma's old trick to test the temperature... sprinkle the heated water on your forearm. If it's neither too hot nor too cold, the temperature is just right.

Oh, What a Beautiful Morning!

Overnight Egg & Cheese Casserole

Rosemary Trezza
Winter Springs, FL

A co-worker shared this recipe with me many years ago. Since then, I have made this casserole for family & friends...they have always loved it and requested the recipe. I have changed a few ingredients to suit our family's tastes. It is so easy to make and serve!

1/2 lb. cooked ham, diced
6 slices white bread, cubed
8-oz. pkg. shredded sharp
    Cheddar cheese

3-1/2 c. milk
1 t. salt
6 eggs, beaten
1/4 c. butter, melted

In a large bowl, toss ham and bread together. Add remaining ingredients and mix well. Spoon mixture into a greased 13"x9" baking pan. Cover and refrigerate overnight. In the morning, uncover and bake at 325 degrees for one hour. Makes 8 servings.

Leftover potatoes make fantastic home fries! In a heavy skillet, heat one to 2 tablespoons oil until sizzling. Add 3 cups cubed cooked potatoes and 1/2 cup chopped onion. Cook for 5 minutes. Turn potatoes over; season with salt, pepper and paprika. Cook another 5 to 10 minutes, to desired doneness.

Autumn Recipes from the Farmhouse

Farmers' Market Breakfast Bake

Sacha George
Kalamazoo, MI

We like a good breakfast casserole or quiche on Sunday mornings! This recipe is a little of both. I like to add fresh vegetables from the farmers' market. Enjoy with fresh fruit on the side.

22-1/2 oz. pkg. frozen
  hashbrown patties, thawed
16-oz. pkg. ground pork
  breakfast sausage
1 to 2 t. olive oil
1 c. chopped fresh vegetables
  like asparagus, green onion,
  carrot, and/or cauliflower

salt, pepper, onion powder and
  garlic powder to taste
8 eggs, beaten
1/4 to 1/2 c. half-and-half
1/2 c. shredded Colby Jack,
  Cheddar or Gouda cheese

Arrange hashbrowns in a single layer in the bottom of a buttered 3-quart casserole dish. Set dish in oven at 375 degrees while preheating. Brown sausage in a skillet over medium heat; drain and set aside sausage. Wipe out skillet; add olive oil. Sauté vegetables; sprinkle with seasonings and set aside. Remove casserole dish from oven; layer sausage and vegetables over hashbrowns. In a bowl, whisk together eggs, half-and-half and cheese; pour over vegetables in dish. Bake, uncovered, at 375 degrees for 30 minutes, or until eggs are set in the center. Makes 8 servings.

Make the most of your front porch! A porch swing, rocking chairs, comfy pillows and hanging baskets of fall flowers create a cozy place for family & friends to chat and enjoy the crisp air.

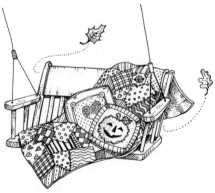

Oh, What a Beautiful Morning!

Clovia Coffee Cake

Diana Krol
Hutchinson, KS

When I was a student at Kansas State University, I lived in the 4-H scholarship house, Clovia. This coffee cake was served for breakfast every Saturday morning. It later became one of my family's favorites, too. Especially good with cold milk, or hot coffee and tea.

2 c. all-purpose flour
2 t. baking powder
1 c. sugar
1-1/2 t. salt

1 egg, beaten
3/4 c. milk
1/2 c. oil

In a large bowl, stir together flour, baking powder, sugar and salt; set aside. In a separate bowl, whisk together egg, milk and oil; add to flour mixture and mix well. Pour batter into an oiled 9"x9" baking pan. Spread Topping over batter. Bake at 375 degrees for 30 minutes, or until cake tests done with a toothpick. Serve warm. Makes 8 to 10 servings.

Topping:

1/2 c. sugar
2 T. all-purpose flour
2 t. cinnamon

1/4 t. salt
1/4 c. butter

Stir together sugar, flour, cinnamon and salt. Cut in butter with a fork until mixture resembles small peas.

Pick up some sturdy vintage mugs
at tag sales for serving hot beverages.
They hold the heat well...wonderful
for warming chilly hands!

Autumn Recipes from the Farmhouse

Joy's Biscuits & Sausage Gravy

Stevie Bowman
Christiansburg, VA

This recipe was passed down from my mother. Every Sunday morning when I was growing up, the smell of Mom's biscuits & gravy woke me up bright and early. For years, I asked Mom to share this recipe with me...the only problem was, she didn't have an actual recipe! She always told me to add a little of this & a little of that. After many years of trial & error, she finally perfected the amounts of the ingredients to create this recipe! This recipe will be passed down for many generations to come.

3 slices bacon
1/2 lb. mild ground pork sausage
1/4 c. all-purpose flour

3 c. whole milk
salt and pepper to taste

Prepare Joy's Biscuits. While biscuits are baking, cook bacon in a skillet over medium heat until crisp. Set aside bacon on paper towels, reserving drippings in skillet. (Add crumbled bacon to finished gravy, or reserve for another use.) Add sausage to drippings and cook until browned, breaking it up with a fork as it cooks. Sprinkle with flour; stir until mixed in well. Add milk, salt and pepper. Cook over medium heat, stirring often to prevent sticking, until gravy begins to boil. Reduce heat to medium-low. Simmer, stirring often, until heated through and to desired consistency. If gravy is too thick, add more milk. Serve Sausage Gravy with split biscuits. Serves 6 to 7.

Joy's Biscuits:

1/2 c. butter
2-1/2 c. self-rising flour

1 c. whole milk

With a pastry blender, cut butter into flour. Stir in milk. Turn dough onto a lightly floured surface. With floured hands, pat dough to 1/2-inch thick. Cut with a floured biscuit cutter. Place biscuits on a greased baking sheet. For crusty sides, place biscuits one inch apart; for soft sides, have biscuits touching. Bake at 450 degrees for 15 to 20 minutes, until lightly golden.

Oh, What a Beautiful Morning!

Cinnamon-Sugar Cow Pies

Lisa Wood
Princeton, MN

I laugh when I announce these cinnamon-sugar biscuits at early morning breakfasts on our little farm of 16 head of cattle. I came up with this one morning and asked my 5-year-old what we should call them. He looked at them and said, "Mom, they look like cow pies!" and the name stuck!

16.3-oz. tube refrigerated flaky
   layered biscuits, divided
2/3 c. sugar
2/3 c. brown sugar, packed

2 t. cinnamon
5 T. butter, melted
Garnish: additional butter

Separate 4 biscuits from tube; seal remaining biscuits in a plastic zipping bag and refrigerate for another meal. Gently separate biscuit layers, making 2 or 3 layers per biscuit. Mix sugars and cinnamon in a bowl. Dip both sides of biscuit layers into melted butter; dredge both sides in sugar mixture. Place on an aluminum foil-lined baking sheet. Bake at 350 degrees for 13 to 15 minutes, until bubbly, golden and slightly puffed. Serve with additional butter. Serves 4.

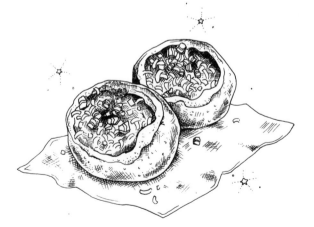

For a special brunch, spoon individual portions of a savory egg casserole into toasty bread bowls. Cut the tops off round crusty bread loaves, hollow them out and brush with olive oil. Pop the bowls and lids into a 400-degree oven for 5 to 10 minutes, until crisp and golden.

Cornmeal Buttermilk Waffles

Zoe Bennett
Columbia, SC

These old-fashioned waffles are delicious! Mom gave me the recipe from a booklet she got back in the 1970s. Serve with butter and maple syrup, or topped with creamed chicken for brunch.

1-1/2 c. water
1/2 c. yellow cornmeal
3 T. butter
3 eggs, separated
3/4 c. buttermilk

1 c. all-purpose flour
2 t. baking powder
1/2 t. baking soda
1 T. sugar
1/2 t. salt

In a saucepan over medium heat, bring water to a boil. Add cornmeal, stirring until smooth. Stir in butter until melted; remove from heat and let stand until slightly cooled. Beat in egg yolks; add buttermilk. Beat well and set aside. In a bowl, combine flour, baking powder, baking soda, sugar and salt. Add cornmeal mixture; stir just until moistened. In another bowl, beat egg whites to stiff peaks with an electric mixer on high speed. Gently fold egg whites into batter, stirring just until blended. Pour 1/2 cup batter per waffle into a preheated, greased waffle iron. Bake according to manufacturer's directions. Makes 4 waffles.

Carve an extra Jack-o'-Lantern or 2 and deliver it to elderly neighbors so they can enjoy some Halloween fun... what a neighborly gesture!

Oh, What a Beautiful Morning!

Cranberry-Date Spread

Nancy Kaiser
York, SC

This spread is great on homemade rolls and biscuits, or on toast for breakfast in the morning. I make this every Thanksgiving and Christmas.

1 c. water
1 c. sugar
12-oz. pkg. fresh cranberries,
    rinsed

4-oz. pkg. chopped dates
1/2 c. chopped walnuts
    or pecans

In a medium saucepan, combine water and sugar; stir to dissolve sugar. Bring to a boil over medium heat. Add cranberries and dates; return to a boil. Reduce heat to medium-low. Simmer gently for about 10 minutes, stirring occasionally. Remove from heat and cool; stir in nuts. Cover and refrigerate up to 2 weeks. Makes about 3 cups.

Peanut Butter Toast Spread

Crystal Shook
Catawba, NC

Delicious on hot buttered toast! Good on pancakes or waffles instead of syrup, too.

2 c. brown sugar, packed
1 c. water
1 t. maple extract

2 c. creamy peanut butter
16-oz. jar marshmallow creme

In a large saucepan, combine brown sugar, water and maple extract. Bring to a boil over medium heat. Add peanut butter and marshmallow creme; beat until smooth. Cool; cover and refrigerate. Makes about 5 cups.

I'm so glad I live in a world
where there are Octobers.

–Lucy Maud Montgomery

Turkey-Vegetable Hashbrown Quiche

JoAnn
Gooseberry Patch

By the end of Thanksgiving weekend, we all get just a little tired of turkey. I found this recipe that's a great change from the usual turkey casseroles or sandwiches...we enjoy it for either breakfast or dinner. If you have leftover cooked veggies from Thanksgiving, you can use them too.

1 egg, beaten
3/4 t. salt, divided
2 c. frozen shredded hashbrown
   potatoes, thawed
2 c. frozen mixed vegetables,
   thawed

1/2 c. cooked turkey, diced
5 eggs
1 c. milk
Optional: 1 c. shredded Cheddar
   or Swiss cheese
2 T. sliced almonds

Whisk together egg and 1/4 teaspoon salt in a large bowl. Add hashbrowns; mix well. Press evenly into bottom and sides of a greased 9" deep-dish pie plate. Bake at 375 degrees for 5 minutes. Spread vegetables evenly in crust; top with turkey. Whisk together eggs, milk and remaining salt in another bowl; carefully pour over turkey. Sprinkle with cheese, if using, and almonds. Set pie plate on center oven rack. Bake, uncovered, at 375 degrees for about 45 minutes, until center is almost set and a knife tip inserted near center comes out clean. Let stand 5 minutes; cut into wedges. Makes 6 servings.

Whip up some cozy throws in bright red or russet plaid fleece...
simply snip fringe all around the edges. They're so easy,
you can make one for each member of the family in no time
at all! Perfect for snuggling while sipping on hot chocolate.

Oh, What a Beautiful Morning!

Pumpkin White Hot Chocolate
Megan Fordyce
Fairchance, PA

A perfect hot pumpkin drink for a crisp fall day! Add a pinch of nutmeg or cloves if you like it a bit spicier.

3-1/2 c. milk
1 c. canned pumpkin
1 c. white chocolate chips

1/4 c. sugar
1 t. cinnamon
Garnish: whipped cream

In a saucepan over medium heat, combine all ingredients except garnish. Cook and stir until chocolate melts and mixture is heated through, but not boiling. Ladle into mugs and top with whipped cream. Makes 4 servings.

Start off a tailgating Saturday right...invite friends to join you for breakfast! Keep it simple, with a make-ahead breakfast casserole, baskets of sweet rolls and a fresh fruit salad. Add mugs of hot coffee and cocoa if it's chilly, or cold cider if the weather turns balmy. It's all about food and friends!

Autumn Recipes
from the Farmhouse

Aunt Jennifer's Farmers' Casserole

Monica Britt
Fairdale, WV

This past summer, we spent our family vacation driving over 20 hours (each way!) to Minnesota to visit my Uncle Earl and Aunt Jennifer. Aunt Jennifer served us the most delightful breakfasts...she is the best hostess I know! When she has lots of company, she doubles this recipe, using a 3-quart dish. It serves 12 and still bakes for 40 to 45 minutes.

3 c. frozen shredded hashbrown potatoes
3/4 c. shredded Monterey Jack cheese with jalapeño peppers, or Cheddar cheese
1 c. cooked ham or Canadian bacon, diced

2/3 c. green onions, chopped
4 eggs, beaten
1-1/2 c. milk, or 12-oz. can evaporated milk
1/8 t. salt
1/8 t. pepper

Arrange hashbrowns evenly in the bottom of a 2-quart casserole dish coated with non-stick cooking spray. Sprinkle with cheese, ham or bacon and onions; set aside. In a large bowl, whisk together eggs, milk, salt and pepper; pour over hashbrown mixture. Bake, uncovered, at 350 degrees for 40 to 45 minutes, until a knife tip inserted in the center comes out clean. Let stand for 5 minutes; serve. Makes 6 servings.

Treat yourself to a buttery slice of cinnamon toast. Spread softened butter generously on one side of toasted white bread and sprinkle with cinnamon-sugar. Broil for one to 2 minutes, until bubbly and golden.

Oh, What a Beautiful Morning!

Faith's Banana Pancakes

Wendy Jo Minotte
Duluth, MN

This recipe has been a favorite ever since a friend shared it with me years ago. Enjoy!

1-1/2 c. all-purpose flour
2/3 c. whole-wheat flour
1 t. baking powder
4 ripe bananas, mashed
2 eggs, beaten

1/4 c. sugar
1-1/2 c. milk
Garnish: butter, pure maple
  syrup

In a large bowl, whisk together flours and baking powder; set aside. In another bowl, combine remaining ingredients except garnish; mix well. Add flour mixture; mix until combined but don't overmix. For each pancake, pour 1/4 cup batter onto a preheated, greased griddle over medium heat. Cook until beginning to bubble around the edges; flip and cook for one more minute. Serve warm with butter and maple syrup. Makes 16 pancakes.

Sourdough Buckwheat Pancakes

Melanie Lowe
Dover, DE

This overnight pancake batter is so handy! When Mom made pancakes for us on busy mornings, this was her secret.

1 t. active dry yeast
2 c. warm water, 110 to
  115 degrees, divided
1 T. honey

1 T. oil
1/2 t. salt
1-1/2 c. buckwheat flour
1/2 c. whole-wheat flour

The night before, in a large bowl, dissolve yeast in 1/2 cup warm water. Add honey and let stand about 5 minutes, until bubbly. Add oil, salt, remaining water and flours. Beat until blended; cover and let rise overnight. In the morning, stir down batter. Pour batter by 1/3 cupfuls onto a hot greased griddle; cook until golden on both sides. Makes 10 small pancakes.

Autumn Recipes
from the Farmhouse

Apple-Stuffed French Toast

Brenda Cook
Uniontown, OH

I started making this French toast one fall, after my whole family (including my young twins, husband and parents) went apple picking at a local orchard. We always picked many more apples than we needed...we wanted the fun to last forever! Since this is assembled the night before, it's a snap to put a warm and fragrant breakfast on the table!

5 firm apples, peeled, cored
   and sliced
1/2 c. water
1 t. cinnamon
1 t. sugar
3 T. butter
3/4 c. brown sugar, packed
3 T. light corn syrup

Optional: 1 c. chopped pecans
12 slices firm white bread,
   divided
3 eggs, beaten
1-1/4 c. milk
1 t. vanilla extract
1/4 t. nutmeg

Combine apples and water in a skillet over medium heat. Simmer for 4 to 5 minutes; drain. Sprinkle apples with cinnamon and sugar; set aside. In same skillet, combine butter, brown sugar and corn syrup. Cook over medium heat until bubbly. Stir in nuts, if using; pour into a buttered 13"x9" baking pan. Arrange 6 slices of bread in pan in a single layer; spoon apples over bread. Arrange remaining bread slices over apples, like "sandwiches." In a large bowl, whisk together eggs, milk, vanilla and nutmeg; pour over bread. Cover and refrigerate until morning. Bake, uncovered, at 350 degrees for 45 minutes. Cut each "sandwich" diagonally; serve with warm Vanilla Syrup. Makes 12 servings.

Vanilla Syrup:

1 c. water
1/2 c. sugar
1 T. cornstarch

2 T. butter
1 t. vanilla extract

Combine water, sugar and cornstarch in a small saucepan. Cook until boiling. Remove from heat; stir in butter and vanilla.

Warming
Soups &
Breads

Autumn Recipes from the Farmhouse

Garden Vegetable Soup

Mary Patenaude
Griswold, CT

This soup is a great way to enjoy the last of the vegetables in the garden.

1/2 c. onion, chopped
1/2 c. celery, chopped
2 T. oil
4 c. chicken broth
4 c. tomatoes, chopped
1-1/2 c. green beans, cut into
    1/2-inch pieces
3/4 c. carrots, peeled and sliced

1 t. sugar
1 t. dried basil
1 bay leaf, crumbled
2 c. zucchini, sliced
1-1/2 c. okra, sliced
1 c. corn, cut off the cob
salt and pepper to taste

In a large stockpot over medium heat, sauté onion and celery in oil until tender. Add chicken broth, tomatoes, beans, carrots, sugar and herbs. Bring to a boil; reduce heat to medium-low. Cover and simmer for 5 minutes, or until carrots are fork-tender. Add remaining vegetables; season with salt and pepper. Simmer for another 10 minutes, or until vegetables are tender. Makes 10 to 12 servings.

Still too warm for a fire in the fireplace? Give it a welcoming autumn glow...fill it with pots of flame-colored orange and yellow mums.

Warming Soups & Breads

Sharon's White Chicken Chili
Sharon Jones
Oklahoma City, OK

This is the best-tasting white chili I have ever had...yummy!
Just add some tortilla chips for a scrumptious meal. If spice
needs to be toned down, add some sour cream to taste.

3 boneless, skinless chicken
   breasts, cooked and shredded
2 15-1/2 oz. cans Great Northern
   or navy beans
2 15-1/2 oz. cans pinto beans

3 c. shredded sharp Cheddar
   cheese
2 c. whipping cream
7-oz. can chipotle peppers in
   adobo sauce, divided

In a 5-quart slow cooker, combine chicken, undrained beans, cheese, cream and half of peppers in sauce, or to taste. (Reserve remaining peppers for another use.) Stir gently. Cover and cook on low setting for 5 hours. Serves 8.

Harvest Cornbread
Amanda Johnson
Marysville, OH

This is the perfect pairing for any hearty soup or stew recipe.
Very easy and versatile...my whole family loves it!

3/4 c. yellow cornmeal
1-1/4 c. all-purpose flour
2 t. baking powder
1 t. salt

1/4 t. nutmeg
1 c. milk
1/2 c. sugar
1/2 c. butter, melted

In a bowl, blend cornmeal, flour, baking powder, salt and nutmeg. Stir in remaining ingredients, just until moistened. Do not overmix. Pour batter into a greased 9" round cake pan. Bake at 400 degrees for 25 minutes, or until a wooden toothpick inserted into the center tests clean. Cut into wedges; serve warm. Makes 6 servings.

A quick fall craft...hot glue large
acorn caps onto magnets
for whimsical fridge magnets.

Autumn Recipes
from the Farmhouse

Roasted Butternut Squash Soup

Sharon Tillman
Hampton, VA

This soup is delicious! I like to begin our Thanksgiving dinner with small cups of soup, dressed up with a drizzle of cream and a sprinkle of toasted seeds.

1 large butternut squash, peeled, seeded and cubed
2 russet potatoes, peeled and cubed
3 T. extra-virgin olive oil, divided
salt and pepper to taste
1 T. butter
1 onion, chopped
1 stalk celery, thinly sliced
1 to 2 carrots, peeled and chopped
1 T. fresh thyme, snipped
4 c. low-sodium chicken broth

In a large bowl, combine butternut squash and potatoes; drizzle with 2 tablespoons olive oil. Season with salt and pepper. Toss to coat well; spread evenly on a 15"x10" jelly-roll pan. Bake at 400 degrees for 25 minutes, or until fork-tender; cool. Meanwhile, in a large pot over medium heat, melt butter with remaining oil. Add onion, celery and carrots; cook until softened, 7 to 10 minutes. Season with salt, pepper and thyme. Add baked squash mixture and chicken broth; simmer for 10 minutes. Use an immersion blender to blend soup until creamy. May also process soup in a blender, working in batches. Serves 4 to 6.

If you like toasted pumpkin seeds, try toasting winter squash seeds too! Rinse seeds and pat dry, toss with olive oil, spread on a baking sheet and sprinkle with salt. Bake at 350 degrees for 10 to 15 minutes, until crisp.

Warming Soups & Breads

Fresh Garden Zucchini Chowder

Bethi Hendrickson
Danville, PA

A family favorite! Use canned diced tomatoes if ripe tomatoes aren't in season.

1/4 c. butter
2 carrots, peeled and thinly sliced
1 to 2 T. garlic, chopped
1/4 c. all-purpose flour
3 c. chicken broth
4 c. tomatoes, cubed

2 c. fresh or frozen corn
1 zucchini, diced
1 t. dried basil
1 c. fat-free half-and-half
1 c. shredded Cheddar cheese

In a large soup pot, melt butter over medium heat. Add carrots and garlic; cook until carrots are tender. Sprinkle with flour; cook and stir until smooth and golden. Cook over low heat for 3 minutes, stirring often, until thickened. Add chicken broth, tomatoes, corn, zucchini and basil. Simmer over low heat for 20 minutes, or until zucchini is tender, stirring often. Add half-and-half and cheese. Simmer for another 10 minutes, stirring often, until heated through and cheese is melted. Serves 8 to 10.

Keep an eye open at tag sales for big, old-fashioned enamelware stockpots. They're just right for cooking up farmhouse-size portions of soup.

Autumn Recipes from the Farmhouse

Savory Pork Stew

Shirley Howie
Foxboro, MA

A hearty, comforting slow-cooker stew that's perfect for the cooler days of autumn and winter. It is a no-fuss family dinner that is sure to please...leftovers are every bit as delicious the next day!

2 lbs. boneless pork, cut into
    1-inch cubes
4 c. chicken or vegetable broth
14-1/2 oz. can stewed tomatoes
3/4 c. onion, chopped
3/4 c. green pepper, chopped
2 stalks celery, chopped

1/3 c. low-sodium soy sauce
1 T. chili powder
1/2 t. garlic powder
1/2 t. pepper
1/3 c. cornstarch
1/3 c. cold water
cooked egg noodles

In a slow cooker, combine all ingredients except cornstarch, cold water and noodles. Mix gently. Cover and cook on low setting for 8 hours. In a cup, mix together cornstarch and water until smooth; gradually stir into soup. Cover and cook on high setting for 30 minutes, or until slightly thickened. Serve in bowls, ladled over cooked noodles. Makes 8 servings.

All-Day Apple Butter

Joyceann Dreibelbis
Wooster, OH

This is delicious and simple to make using a slow cooker. You may want to adjust the sugar to taste, depending on the sweetness of the apples used. I like to use Jonagold apples.

5-1/2 lbs. apples, peeled, cored
    and finely chopped
4 c. sugar

2 to 3 t. cinnamon
1/4 t. ground cloves
1/4 t. salt

Place apples in a 4-quart slow cooker. Combine sugar, spices and salt; sprinkle over apples and mix well. Cover and cook on high setting for one hour. Reduce heat to low; cover and cook for 9 to 11 hours, until thickened and dark brown, stirring occasionally. As mixture begins to thicken, stir more often, to prevent sticking. Uncover; cook on low setting one hour longer. If desired, stir with a wire whisk until smooth. Spoon into plastic freezer containers. Cover and refrigerate or freeze. Makes 4 pints.

Warming Soups & Breads

Anne's Minnesota Wild Rice Soup

Andrea Czarniecki
Northville, MI

*A wonderful chilly-day dinner. It warms you up right away...
comfort in a bowl! My special friend Anne shared it with me
years ago and I think of her every time I make it.*

2 c. wild rice, uncooked
1/2 to 1 lb. bacon
1 c. onion, chopped
3/4 c. celery, chopped
1/2 c. carrot, peeled and chopped

1/2 c. green pepper, chopped
1-1/4 c. water
3 10-3/4 oz. cans cream of
   mushroom soup
2 14-oz. cans chicken broth

Cook rice according to package directions. Meanwhile, in a skillet over medium heat, cook bacon until crisp. Set aside bacon on paper towels; reserve one tablespoon drippings in skillet. Add onion, celery, carrot and green pepper to reserved drippings; cook for 3 to 4 minutes. Stir in water; simmer until vegetables are soft. In a soup pot, whisk together mushroom soup and chicken broth until smooth. Add cooked wild rice, vegetable mixture and crumbled bacon; stir well. Simmer over low heat until heated through. Makes 6 to 8 servings.

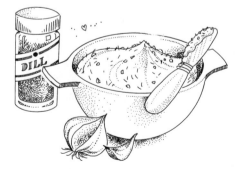

Herb butter is delicious on fresh-baked breads. Simply blend chopped fresh herbs into softened butter and spoon into a crock. Choose from parsley, dill, tarragon and chives, or create your own herb garden mixture.

Meatball Soup

Doreen Knapp
Stanfordville, NY

This is a great, hearty soup! My two boys love it any time of year with crusty bread and a fresh tossed salad.

1 egg
1 lb. ground beef
1/2 c. Italian-seasoned dry
   bread crumbs
2 T. chopped fresh parsley,
   or 1 T. dried parsley
1 T. grated Parmigiano-Reggiano
   cheese
1 clove garlic, minced

1/2 t. salt
1/4 t. pepper
10-1/2 oz. can beef broth
10 c. water
6-oz. pkg. thin egg noodles,
   uncooked
Garnish: additional chopped
   parsley, grated cheese

In a large bowl, beat egg lightly. Add beef, bread crumbs, parsley, cheese, garlic, salt and pepper. Mix well; form into one-inch meatballs, using your hands or a small scoop. In a large soup pot, bring beef broth and water to a boil. Add meatballs and simmer for 5 minutes. With a slotted spoon, remove meatballs to a bowl; return broth mixture to a boil. Add egg noodles; cook according to package directions, stirring occasionally. Return meatballs to soup and warm through, about one to 2 minutes. Ladle soup into bowls; top with parsley and grated cheese. Serves 8.

Straw shopping totes from the thrift store make whimsical holders for autumn mums...just slip them over fence posts and fill with flowers.

Warming Soups & Breads

Quick Vegetable Beef Soup

Carolyn Deckard
Bedford, IN

This is one of my favorite soups and it's so easy to fix. Soup is my favorite thing to eat in this cool weather...something to warm us up. Serve with French bread for a delicious meal.

1-1/2 lbs. lean ground beef
1 c. onion, chopped
2 cloves garlic, finely chopped
28-oz. can diced tomatoes
6 c. water

6 cubes beef bouillon
1/4 t. pepper
1/2 c. orzo pasta, uncooked
1-1/2 c. frozen peas, carrots & corn vegetable blend

In a large saucepan over medium-high heat, cook beef, onion and garlic until beef is browned, stirring to crumble; drain. In a blender or food processor, process tomatoes with juice until smooth. Add tomatoes to beef mixture along with water, bouillon cubes and pepper. Bring to a boil; reduce heat to low. Simmer, uncovered, for 20 minutes. Stir in orzo and vegetables. Simmer an additional 15 minutes, stirring occasionally, until tender. Makes 6 servings.

Create a spooky greeting for trick-or-treaters...it's simple!
Paint dried bottle gourds white and use a black felt tip pen
to add a ghostly face. Line up several on the porch
or along the mantel.

Autumn Recipes from the Farmhouse

Kielbasa, Turnip & Cabbage Soup

Gail Blain
Grand Island, NE

*I love that this recipe uses a couple of the staples of
my fall garden...cabbage and turnips!*

2 T. olive oil
1-1/4 lbs. Kielbasa sausage,
    cut into 1-inch slices
1 onion, chopped
2 cloves garlic, pressed
1 c. regular or non-alcoholic
    beer, room temperature
4 c. chicken broth

2 c. tomato purée
1 lb. turnips, peeled and chopped
2 stalks celery, chopped
1 T. paprika
1/2 t. ground allspice
salt and pepper to taste
1/2 head cabbage, chopped
1/8 t. nutmeg

Heat oil in a large Dutch oven over medium-high heat. Add Kielbasa,
onion and garlic; cook until onion is tender and lightly golden. Add
beer. Cook and stir until liquid cooks down slightly, scraping up all the
browned bits. Add chicken broth, tomato purée, turnips, celery and
seasonings. Cook, partially covered, for 5 to 6 minutes. Stir in cabbage
and nutmeg; reduce heat to medium-low. Simmer for one to 2 hours to
combine flavors, stirring occasionally. Serves 6 generously.

The next time you see a roadside stand in the country, stop and take
a look! You're sure to find the freshest fruits & veggies, cut flowers
and homemade goodies like pickles, preserves, pies and cakes...
maybe even fresh bread and creamery butter to go with your soup.

Warming Soups & Breads

Zucchini Bread

Denise Webb
Sylvania, GA

I got this recipe years ago at a fruit & vegetable farm and it's the only zucchini bread I make. Moist and flavorful...it's the best! It makes two loaves, so I can share one with a friend, or freeze for later.

3 eggs, well beaten	3 c. all-purpose flour
2 c. sugar	1 t. baking powder
1 c. oil	1 t. baking soda
1 T. vanilla extract	2 t. cinnamon
2 c. zucchini, shredded	1 t. salt

In a large bowl, whisk together together eggs, sugar, oil and vanilla. Stir in zucchini; set aside. In another bowl, mix together remaining ingredients and add to zucchini mixture, stirring well. Divide batter between 2 greased and floured 9"x5" loaf pans. Bake at 350 degrees for 40 to 45 minutes, until done when tested with a toothpick. Makes 2 loaves.

Country Butter

Diana Chaney
Olathe, KS

A friend shared this recipe with me. It's easy to spread on bread...even on toast! Great for pan-frying too.

1 c. butter, room temperature	2 c. olive oil

Place butter in a large bowl. Beat with an electric mixer on low to medium speed until fluffy. While still beating, drizzle olive oil into bowl; beat until well mixed. Mixture will be very thick. Transfer to a container; cover and refrigerate overnight before using. Butter will set up yet spread easily. Makes 3 pounds.

I can see the woods in their autumn dress,
the oaks purple, the hickories washed with gold,
the maples and the sumacs luminous with crimson fires.
–Mark Twain

Autumn Recipes from the Farmhouse

October Chili

Glenda Reynolds
Millersport, OH

Every October for the last 35 years, our entire family has gathered for a fall get-together at our little mini-farm, the Reynolds Homestead. It is a time of fun and good food. Paw's famous chili has always been the star of the show. Although Paw is no longer with us, his children and grandchildren continue the tradition...we are happy to share his recipe with you. For the very best flavor, cook over an open fire.

3 lbs. ground beef chuck
1 lb. ground pork
2 white onions, chopped
3 15-1/2 oz. cans dark red chili
   beans, partially drained
15-1/2 oz. can hot chili beans
3 10-3/4 oz. cans tomato soup
4 c. homemade or store-bought
   tomato juice

3 jalapeño peppers, diced,
   2 with seeds and veins
   removed
1 green pepper, diced
1 red pepper, diced
1 roasted red pepper, diced
chili powder, ground cumin and
   cayenne pepper to taste
1-1/2 t. molasses

Early in the day, brown meats and onions over medium heat in a large Dutch oven; drain. Add remaining ingredients; mix well. Cover and simmer over medium-low to medium heat, stirring occasionally, for 2 hours. Makes 15 to 20 servings.

Quick breads taste best when wrapped and stored overnight at room temperature. They'll slice more easily too.

Warming Soups & Breads

Anne's Corn Chowder

Anne Alesauskas
Minocqua, WI

The bonus with this soup is that it freezes well, so when the corn is in season, I can make an extra-large batch to pull out for meals over the fall and winter.

1 lb. bacon, diced
1 T. olive oil
3/4 c. onion, diced
2 cloves garlic, minced
2 roasted red sweet peppers,
   seeded and diced
1 stalk celery, diced
15-oz. can sliced new potatoes,
   drained

4 c. fresh corn kernels, or
   2 11-oz. cans yellow &
   white corn, drained
1/4 c. all-purpose flour
6 c. chicken broth
juice of 1/2 lime
1/2 c. whipping cream
salt and pepper to taste

In a large stockpot over medium heat, cook bacon until crisp. Remove bacon to drain on paper towels, reserving one tablespoon drippings in pan. Add olive oil, onion, garlic, peppers, celery, potatoes and corn. Sauté for 6 to 8 minutes, until vegetables are tender. Sprinkle with flour; cook and stir for about 3 minutes. While stirring, slowly add broth and mix well. Using an immersion blender, blend for a few pulses, just enough to break up some of the potatoes and vegetables, but not until completely smooth. This will aid in the thickening process. Reduce heat to low. Stir in lime juice and cream; season with salt and pepper. Simmer over low heat for 20 minutes and serve. Makes 6 to 8 servings.

Whip up some herbed crackers for sprinkling on soup. Toss together 1-1/2 cups oyster crackers, 1-1/2 tablespoons melted butter, 1/4 teaspoon dried thyme and 1/4 teaspoon garlic powder. Spread on a baking sheet. Bake at 350 degrees for about 10 minutes, until crunchy and golden.

Autumn Recipes from the Farmhouse

Best-Ever Ham & Bean Soup

Lori Ledbetter
Gaston, IN

When out-of-town guests come to visit, rather than trying to schedule everyone they'd like to visit individually, plan a "Soup Day Open House" so everyone can come to see them! Set out a simple meal of soup served in slow cookers, fresh breads and cookies. Everyone can come & go as they please and enjoy a delicious meal without a lot of effort. Who knows, maybe it will become a tradition! Serve with your favorite cornbread.

1 onion, chopped
1 T. olive oil
48-oz. jar Great Northern beans
3 c. chicken broth
4-oz. can diced green chiles,
    drained

1 c. cooked ham, chopped
3/4 t. dried oregano
1/2 t. garlic powder
1 t. ground cumin
1/4 t. white pepper
Optional: sliced green onions

In a large stockpot over medium heat, sauté onion in oil. Add undrained beans and remaining ingredients except optional green onions. Bring to a boil; reduce heat to medium-low. Simmer for 35 to 45 minutes, stirring often. Serve soup garnished with onions, if desired. Makes 6 servings.

Start a delicious soup supper tradition on Halloween night. Soup stays simmering hot while you hand out treats, and it isn't too filling, leaving more room to nibble on goodies!

Warming Soups & Breads

Bacon, Bean & Sweet Pepper Soup

Vickie
Gooseberry Patch

My family loves this bean soup! Full of veggies and bacon,
it's hearty and filling. I serve it with corn fritters...we like
to dunk them in our soup bowls.

1-1/2 c. dried navy beans,
  rinsed and sorted
5 to 6 slices bacon
2 c. onions, chopped
2 c. red and/or green peppers,
  chopped
1 c. carrots, peeled and chopped
4 cloves garlic, minced

1 t. sugar
1 t. onion powder
1 t. garlic powder
1/4 t. pepper
1/8 t. cayenne pepper
3 14-1/2 oz. cans chicken
  broth, divided
Garnish: chopped fresh parsley

In a Dutch oven, cover beans with water to 2 inches above beans. Bring to a boil over high heat; cook for 2 minutes. Remove from heat; cover and let stand for one hour. Drain; return to Dutch oven and set aside. Meanwhile, cook bacon in a skillet over medium heat until crisp. Remove bacon to a paper towel; reserving drippings in skillet. Add remaining ingredients except chicken broth and garnish to drippings; sauté for 10 minutes, or until onion is golden. Stir in one can broth, scraping pan to loosen any browned bits. Transfer onion mixture to beans in pan; add remaining broth. Bring to a boil; reduce heat to medium-low. Cover and simmer for one hour, or until beans are tender. Transfer 3 cups of soup to a blender; process until smooth and return to pan. Heat through; stir in crumbled bacon and parsley. Serves 8.

Top steamy bowls of soup with crunchy cheese toasts. Cut bread with a mini cookie cutter and brush lightly with olive oil. Place on a broiler pan and broil for 2 to 3 minutes, until golden. Turn over; sprinkle with freshly shredded Parmesan cheese. Broil another 2 to 3 minutes, until cheese melts. Yum!

Wisconsin Cheddar Cheese Soup

*Barbara Klein
Newburgh, IN*

My family loves this soup! It's a real warmer-upper after we've come in from a chilly afternoon of raking leaves or doing other activities outdoors.

1 c. celery, chopped
3/4 c. carrots, peeled and
   chopped
1-1/2 c. water
1/4 c. butter
1/2 c. onion, chopped

3/4 c. all-purpose flour
4 c. milk
2-1/2 c. chicken broth
16-oz. pkg. shredded Cheddar
   cheese
salt and pepper to taste

In a small saucepan over medium heat, combine celery, carrots and water. Bring to a boil; reduce heat to medium-low and simmer until vegetables are tender. Meanwhile, melt butter in a soup pot over medium heat. Add onion and cook until tender. Stir in flour and milk; cook and stir until thickened. Stir in chicken broth, cheese and vegetable mixture with liquid. Season with salt and pepper. Cook and stir over low heat until cheese is melted and soup is smooth. Serves 6.

Celebrate autumn...take a family nature walk and collect some pine cones to make a treat for the birds. Tie a hanging string to the top of each pine cone, then spread with peanut butter mixed with cornmeal and roll in birdseed. Birds will love it!

Warming Soups & Breads

Aunt Frankie's Oat Scones

Marcia Shaffer
Conneaut Lake, PA

My Aunt Frankie was a wonderful cook and always had goodies around. On chilly days, these simple scones were quick & easy when company came, served with a pat of butter and a cup of hot tea.

1 c. all-purpose flour
1 c. old-fashioned oats,
   uncooked
1/2 t. salt
1/2 t. baking soda

1 t. cream of tartar
1 T. plus 1/4 t. sugar
1/4 c. shortening or lard
1/2 c. milk

Combine all ingredients in a large bowl; mix well. Roll out dough into a circle on a lightly floured surface, about 1-1/2 inches thick. Cut into 6 to 8 wedges; place on a greased baking sheet. Bake at 425 degrees for 15 minutes, or until a toothpick tests done. Makes 6 to 8 scones.

Raspberry Butter

Jill Ball
Highland, UT

We are lucky enough to live by a beautiful raspberry farm, where we buy some of the most wonderful raspberries every fall. This recipe is a great alternative to jam. It's scrumptious on hot rolls, toast, pancakes and even right off a spoon!

8-oz. pkg. cream cheese,
   softened
1/2 c. butter, softened

1 c. powdered sugar
1 t. vanilla extract
1 c. fresh raspberries, mashed

In a bowl, combine all ingredients except raspberries; blend well. Fold in berries. Cover and refrigerate overnight before serving. Makes 24 servings.

A basket of homemade scones
with a jar of creamy spread
makes a tasty gift.

Autumn Recipes
from the Farmhouse

Homestyle Beef Stew & Savory Biscuits

Tammy Rowe
Bellevue, OH

*This stew is excellent served with my savory biscuits...
a real tummy-warming meal!*

1 lb. stew beef cubes	1/4 c. catsup
2/3 c. all-purpose flour	4 carrots, peeled and sliced
1-1/2 t. salt	4 potatoes, peeled and sliced
1 t. pepper	4 stalks celery, chopped
1 t. paprika	1 c. onion, coarsely chopped
1/4 c. oil	3 bay leaves
46-oz. can beef broth	1 c. frozen petite peas

Place beef cubes, flour and seasonings in a large plastic zipping bag.
Seal bag; shake until well coated. Heat oil in a soup pot over medium
heat; add contents of bag. Cook and stir until beef is browned. Add beef
broth and catsup. Stir well to loosen any browned bits from pan and
mix in any excess flour. Bring to a boil; cook and stir for one minute.
Add carrots, potatoes, celery, onion and bay leaves. Simmer over low
to medium temperature for 2 hours, stirring occasionally. Discard bay
leaves; stir in peas. Simmer for 10 to 15 minutes. Serves 8 to 10.

Savory Biscuits:

2-1/4 c. biscuit baking mix	2 t. favorite dried herbs
2/3 c. milk	1/2 c. shredded Cheddar cheese

Combine baking mix and milk; stir well. Fold in herbs and cheese. Drop
by spoonfuls onto an ungreased baking sheet. Bake at 450 degrees for
8 to 10 minutes, until golden. Makes 8 biscuits.

Browning meat adds rich color and
flavor. Don't overcrowd the pan...
add cubes or strips in batches,
not all at once.

Warming Soups & Breads

Corn & Butternut Squash Soup
Kay Marone
Des Moines, IA

Garnish with sour cream, if desired.

12 slices bacon, diced
3/4 c. onion, chopped
1 stalk celery, chopped
2 T. all-purpose flour
14-1/2 oz. can chicken broth
6 c. butternut squash, cooked
    and mashed

2 8-3/4 oz. cans cream-style
    corn
2 c. half-and-half
1 T. fresh parsley, minced
1-1/2 t. salt
1/2 t. pepper

In a large saucepan over medium heat, cook bacon until crisp. Remove
bacon to paper towels, reserving 2 tablespoons drippings in pan. Sauté
onion and celery in drippings until tender. Stir in flour until blended.
Gradually stir in chicken broth. Bring to a boil; cook and stir for
2 minutes, or until slightly thickened. Reduce heat to medium. Stir
in crumbled bacon and remaining ingredients. Cook and stir over
medium-low heat until heated through. Makes 8 servings.

Looking for a new garnish for soups? Try some tasty fried sage!
Drop fresh sage leaves, a few at a time, into a skillet of hot oil.
Fry for just a few seconds, until leaves are crisp and bright
green. Drain on a paper towel and sprinkle with salt.

Autumn Recipes from the *Farmhouse*

Stephanie's Chicken Soup

Stephanie Nilsen
Fremont, NE

This is my recipe that I have worked on over the years. Everyone I've served it to loves it! It is very flavorful. Grilled chicken seasoning is the secret ingredient...you're sure to find one in the baking aisle.

2 T. oil
2 carrots, peeled and sliced
2 stalks celery, diced
1 onion, diced
2 boneless, skinless chicken
   breasts

8 c. water
5 T. plus 1 t. chicken soup base
1 T. grilled chicken seasoning
12-oz. pkg. frozen egg noodles,
   uncooked

Heat oil in a large soup kettle over medium heat. Add vegetables; cook and stir until slightly tender. Remove vegetables from pan and set aside. Add chicken breasts; sauté until no longer pink. Remove chicken and set aside. Add water and soup base to pan. Bring to a boil, scraping up browned bits in bottom of pan. Cut chicken into bite-size pieces; return chicken and vegetables to pan. Stir in chicken seasoning; bring mixture to boil. Add frozen noodles and cook for about 20 minutes, until noodles are tender. Makes 8 servings.

Tuck family photos into florist card holders and arrange with colorful mums...what a terrific autumn centerpiece!

Mini Cranberry Corn Muffins
Eleanor Dionne
Beverly, MA

These little gems are a favorite around Thanksgiving or anytime.

2 c. all-purpose flour	1/3 c. chilled butter, sliced
1/2 c. yellow cornmeal	1 egg, beaten
1/2 c. light brown sugar, packed	1 c. milk
2-1/2 t. baking powder	2 t. vanilla extract
1/2 t. salt	1 c. sweetened dried cranberries

In a large bowl, combine flour, cornmeal, brown sugar, baking powder and salt; mix well. Cut in butter with a pastry blender until fine crumbs form; set aside. In another bowl, whisk together egg, milk and vanilla; stir into flour mixture until blended. Fold in cranberries. Spoon batter into 24 paper-lined mini muffin cups, filling to top. Bake at 400 degrees for 25 minutes, or until tops of muffins spring back when touched. Turn out muffins onto a wire rack to cool. Makes 2 dozen.

If you love tailgating, but can't score tickets to the big stadium football game, round up the gang and tailgate at the local Friday-night high school game. Pack a picnic and cheer on your team!

Cabbage Roll Stew

Lisa Dodson
Clinton, KY

When the air begins to turn crisp and cool, this is a family favorite and our go-to soup recipe.

1 lb. ground beef
1 onion, chopped
14-1/2 oz. can sliced carrots, drained
1 medium head cabbage, finely chopped or shredded
1 T. garlic powder
2 c. low-sodium beef broth
28-oz. can tomato sauce

15-oz. can no-sodium-added diced tomatoes
1 t. dried oregano
1 t. dried thyme
1 c. long-cooking brown rice, uncooked
Optional: 1/2 to 1 c. water
1/2 t. salt
1/2 t. pepper

Brown beef in a large soup pot over medium heat, breaking up any large pieces. Remove beef to a bowl and and set aside, reserving 2 tablespoons drippings in pan. Add onion and carrots; sauté for 2 minutes. Add cabbage and garlic powder; cook for 3 to 4 minutes. Stir in beef broth, tomato sauce, diced tomatoes with juice, oregano and thyme. Bring to a light boil. Stir in rice and beef; reduce heat to medium-low. Cover and simmer until rice is cooked, about 25 minutes, stirring occasionally. If soup gets too thick; stir in optional water. Season with salt and pepper. Makes 12 servings.

Pick up a vintage soup tureen at an antique shop or barn sale.
It will add an old-fashioned flair to the dinner table or buffet,
while keeping the soup warm and cozy.

Warming Soups & Breads

Bride's No-Fail Rolls

Susie Taylor
Republic, MO

My mom gave this recipe to me more than 50 years ago when we got married. I can still remember the smell of the rolls in our home. She always used a crock bowl. I still use the crock bowl that she gave me.

1 env. active dry yeast
1 c. very warm water, 110 to
   115 degrees
2 eggs, beaten
1/3 c. sugar

1/3 c. canola oil
1 t. salt
3-1/2 c. all-purpose flour
Garnish: softened butter

In a small bowl, mix yeast and warm water; let stand until yeast is dissolved. In a large bowl, stir together eggs and sugar; add oil and salt. Add yeast mixture; stir well. Add flour, one cup at a time, mixing well. Cover and let rise until double. Drop dough by tablespoons into a lightly greased 13"x9" pan. Let rise until double. Bake at 400 degrees for 20 minutes. Remove rolls from pan while warm, so the bottoms won't get soggy. Spread tops with butter while still warm. Makes about 2 dozen.

Persimmon Butter

Edith Beck
Elk Grove, CA

This is a great way to use up a big crop of persimmons. You use this butter just as you would any apple butter. Recipe can be doubled easily. Makes a wonderful gift at the holidays!

12 very ripe persimmons, peeled,
   halved and seeded
2 T. frozen orange juice
   concentrate

1/4 c. white or brown sugar
1 t. cinnamon
1/4 t. ground cloves

Combine all ingredients in a 3-quart slow cooker; stir. Cover and cook on low setting for 8 hours. Use an immersion blender to purée mixture in slow cooker, or transfer to a blender in small batches and process until smooth and well blended. Transfer to small containers. Cover and refrigerate for 2 weeks, or freeze for longer storage. Makes about 4 cups.

Autumn Recipes from the Farmhouse

Simple Vegetable Soup

Lauren Williams
Mayfield, KY

My mother used to make this vegetable soup whenever the weather turned cold, rainy or windy, or if we were sick or just needed some good stick-to-your-bones food. Served with cornbread crumbled into the soup bowls, eating just doesn't get any better!

16-oz. pkg. frozen garden variety
   mixed vegetables
1 onion, chopped
4 potatoes, peeled and diced
46-oz. can tomato juice
3 c. water
1 T. oil
1 t. salt

Combine all ingredients in a large soup pot. Bring to a boil over high heat; boil for about 20 minutes. Reduce heat to medium-low and simmer for about one hour, stirring occasionally. The longer the soup simmers, the thicker it will get. Makes 6 servings.

Cheddar Cheese & Chive Soup

Gladys Kielar
Whitehouse, OH

Enjoy this simple cheesy soup any time of the year.

14-1/2 oz. can vegetable broth
2 t. fresh chives, chopped
1 t. dried, minced onions
1/4 t. garlic, minced
2 c. shredded Cheddar cheese
1/2 c. milk

In a saucepan, combine vegetable broth, chives, onions and garlic. Bring to a boil over high heat. Add cheese and stir well as it melts. Reduce heat to low; add milk. Stir constantly until heated through. Serves 4.

Paint names on colorful mini gourds for whimsical placecards.

Warming Soups & Breads

Grandmother's Nut Bread

Shannon Reents
Deerfield, OH

*My grandmother was a great cook and baker. I loved it
when she made this nut bread.*

3 c. all-purpose flour	1/2 c. butter, softened
1 T. baking powder	1 c. sugar
1 t. salt	1 egg, well beaten
1 c. chopped walnuts	1-1/4 c. milk

Sift flour into a large bowl. Add baking powder and salt; sift together
3 times. Add nuts and set aside. In another bowl, blend together butter,
sugar and egg; stir in milk. Add butter mixture to flour mixture; stir
just until smooth. Pour batter into a greased 9"x5" loaf pan. Bake at
350 degrees for one hour and 10 minutes. Makes one loaf.

Pumpkin Pie Spread

Kim Hinshaw
Cedar Park, TX

A great hostess gift to give in a small jar...just add a bow!

1 lb. butter	1 t. ground allspice
2 to 3 t. powdered sugar	3/4 t. ground ginger
2 t. cinnamon	1/4 t. salt
1 t. nutmeg	

Place butter in a large bowl; set aside to soften. Sift together powdered
sugar and spices; add to butter. Beat with an electric mixer on low speed
until well blended. Store in an airtight container in refrigerator; serve at
room temperature. Makes one pound.

Take an autumn bike ride...fill the
bike's basket with a thermos of soup
and a loaf of bread. What fun!

Autumn Recipes from the Farmhouse

Kielbasa Lentil Soup

Jessica Kraus
Delaware, OH

One of my favorite cool-weather soups. It's super hearty!
I love to serve this soup with shredded Parmesan cheese,
grated horseradish and crusty bread.

1 lb. dried lentils, rinsed
   and sorted
1/4 c. olive oil
4 c. yellow onions, diced
2 leeks, chopped, white and
   light green parts only
2 cloves garlic, minced
salt and pepper to taste

1 T. fresh thyme, minced
1 t. ground cumin
3 c. celery, diced
3 c. carrots, peeled and diced
12 c. chicken broth
1/4 c. tomato paste
1 lb. Kielbasa sausage, diced

In a large bowl, cover lentils with boiling water. Let stand for
15 minutes; drain and set aside. Heat olive oil in a large stockpot over
medium heat. Sauté onions, leeks, garlic, salt, pepper, thyme and cumin
for 20 minutes, or until onions are translucent and tender. Add celery
and carrots; sauté for another 10 minutes. Stir in chicken broth, tomato
paste and drained lentils; cover and bring to a boil. Reduce heat to
medium-low. Season again with salt and pepper. Simmer, uncovered,
for one hour, or until lentils are tender, stirring occasionally. While soup
is cooking, sauté Kielbasa in a skillet over medium heat until beginning
to brown. Add Kielbasa to the soup; cook an additional 10 minutes.
Makes 10 servings.

Jumping in leaf piles is a not-to-be-
missed part of fall fun! No fallen leaves
in your yard? Ask some neighbors
with a big maple tree for permission
to rake up their leaves...
you'll have a ball!

Warming Soups & Breads

Potato, Ham & Green Bean Soup

Shelley Turner
Boise, ID

This creamy soup can be cooked up in no time at all! We like to sprinkle a little shredded cheese on each bowl before serving.

3-1/2 c. potatoes, peeled
   and diced
1/2 c. celery, diced
1/3 c. onion, chopped
3-1/4 c. chicken broth
14-1/2 oz. can cut green beans,
   drained

1 c. cooked ham, diced
garlic powder, salt and pepper
   to taste
5 T. butter
5 T. all-purpose flour
2 c. whole milk

In a soup pot, combine potatoes, celery, onion and chicken broth. Bring to a boil over high heat. Reduce heat to medium; add green beans, ham and seasonings. Cook until potatoes are tender, about 15 minutes. Meanwhile, in a small saucepan over low heat, melt butter. Whisk in flour; slowly whisk in milk. Cook and stir over medium heat until thickened, 4 to 5 minutes. Stir milk mixture into potato mixture; simmer until heated through. Make 4 to 6 servings.

Use a linoleum craft knife to carve swirling designs in pumpkins.
Since only the outer surface is carved, there's no need to
hollow out the pumpkins...so easy!

Autumn Recipes
from the Farmhouse

Chicken & Vegetable Stew

Leona Krivda
Belle Vernon, PA

This slow-cooker stew is quick & easy...my favorite kind of recipe! My family always enjoys it, along with a side salad and cornbread.

1 lb. boneless, skinless breast, cubed
garlic powder, salt and pepper to taste
14-1/2 oz. can Italian-seasoned diced tomatoes
2 russet potatoes, peeled and cubed
1 c. carrots, peeled and cut into matchsticks
1/2 c. onion, finely chopped

2 4-oz. cans sliced mushrooms, drained
3 cubes chicken bouillon
2 t. sugar
1/2 t. dried basil
1/2 t. dried dill weed
1/4 t. chili powder
1/4 t. pepper
2 T. cornstarch
2 c. cold water

Season chicken cubes lightly with garlic powder, salt and pepper; add to a 4-quart slow cooker. Top with undrained tomatoes; add remaining ingredients except cornstarch and water. Mix gently. Combine cornstarch and water; mix well and stir into mixture in slow cooker. Cover and cook on low setting for 8 to 10 hours. Makes 6 to 8 servings.

Remember to tote along some folding stools when you go camping. There's nothing like sitting around a glowing campfire, stargazing, swapping stories and just savoring time together with family & friends!

Warming Soups & Breads

Turkey Noodle Soup
Stephanie Dardani-D'Esposito
Ravena, NY

*I make this soup every year after Thanksgiving. It stays hot
in the slow cooker on the countertop, and my five kids
help themselves to it all day!*

2 c. cooked turkey, cubed
4 cubes chicken bouillon
2 32-oz. containers chicken
   broth
2 stalks celery, chopped, with
   some leaves included

2 carrots, peeled and chopped
1/2 c. onion, chopped
3 cloves garlic, diced
1 c. narrow egg noodles,
   uncooked

Combine all ingredients except noodles in a 4-quart slow cooker; stir
gently. Cover and cook on high setting for 4 hours. Stir in noodles;
cover and cook for one more hour. Makes 8 servings.

Buttery Crunchy Croutons
Staci Prickett
Montezuma, GA

*This is a great way to use up day-old bread, so don't toss it out...freeze
it instead. For added zest, use a flavored, herbed or cheese bread in
place of plain bread. My favorites for soups & salads are Asiago and
jalapeño cheese bread.*

6 slices favorite Italian or French
   crusty bread, 1-inch thick,
   cut into 1-inch cubes

1/4 c. butter, melted
salt and cracked pepper to taste

Spread bread cubes in a single layer on an ungreased baking sheet.
Drizzle with melted butter; toss until evenly coated. Sprinkle lightly with
salt and pepper; toss again. Bake at 350 degrees for 20 to 30 minutes,
turning croutons twice during baking, until golden and as crunchy as
desired. Makes 6 servings.

Autumn Recipes
from the Farmhouse

Autumn Chili

Bianca Erickson
Hidden Valley Lake, CA

This is my family's comfort food on cold, rainy days. We especially love to eat it next to a crackling fire while chatting about our day and the upcoming holidays.

2 lbs. ground beef
2 15-oz. cans ranch-style beans
8-oz. can tomato sauce
2 c. water
4 roma tomatoes, chopped
3 to 4 cloves garlic, minced

2 T. chili powder, or to taste
2 T. Italian seasoning, or to taste
salt and pepper to taste
red wine vinegar to taste
Optional: shredded Cheddar
   cheese, diced red onions

Brown beef in a skillet over medium heat; drain and add beef to a 5-quart slow cooker. Add beans, tomato sauce, water, tomatoes, garlic and seasonings; stir well. Cover and cook on low setting for 6 to 8 hours. After several hours, taste and add vinegar to taste. Garnish with cheese and/or onions, if desired. Makes 8 servings.

For a country-style welcome, fill a basket with everything that's needed for a simple supper like Autumn Chili and deliver to new neighbors...how thoughtful!

Warming Soups & Breads

Cornbread Bites

Lori Rosenberg
Cleveland, OH

These little morsels are great for folks who like to graze on Thanksgiving Day...easy to pop in your mouth! Excellent alongside a bowl of chili too.

2/3 c. all-purpose flour
1/2 c. yellow cornmeal
1 T. sugar
1-1/2 t. baking powder
1/4 t. salt
1/2 c. shredded sharp Cheddar
  cheese

1/2 c. reduced-fat sour cream
1/4 c. green onions, thinly sliced
18-3/4 oz. can cream-style corn
1/8 t. hot pepper sauce
1 egg, lightly beaten

In a large bowl, combine flour, cornmeal, sugar, baking powder and salt; mix well and set aside. In another bowl, whisk together remaining ingredients; add to flour mixture and stir just until moistened. Divide batter evenly among 12 mini muffin cups coated with non-stick vegetable spray. Bake at 375 degrees for 10 minutes, or until golden. Cool in pan on a wire rack for 2 minutes. Remove muffins from pan and cool completely. Makes one dozen.

If you like your cornbread crisp, prepare it in a vintage sectioned cast-iron skillet. Each wedge of cornbread will bake up with its own golden crust.

Autumn Recipes
from the *Farmhouse*

Potato-Leek Soup

Wendy Meadows
Spring Hill, FL

My kids loved cream of potato soup when they were little. As they grew up and their tastes changed, we added other ingredients to the bowls... crisp bacon crumbles, shredded cheese, snipped chives. If you prefer, a finely diced white or yellow onion can be substituted for the leeks.

1 T. butter
1 to 2 leeks, sliced into thin
   half-moons, white and light
   green parts only
1 c. carrots, peeled and shredded
1/8 t. salt
1/2 lb. russet potatoes, peeled
   and cubed

1/2 lb. redskin or Yukon Gold
   potatoes, peeled and cubed
1 c. white wine or water
12 c. chicken broth
2 c. whipping cream

Melt butter in a large stockpot over medium heat. Stir in leeks and cook for 3 to 4 minutes, stirring occasionally. Add carrots and salt; cook, stirring occasionally, for another 3 to 4 minutes. Add potatoes; continue cooking and stirring for another 5 minutes. Add wine or water; cook for 5 minutes. Add chicken broth and enough water to cover potatoes. Bring to a boil; cook for 5 minutes. Reduce heat to medium-low. Simmer for 30 minutes, or until potatoes are cooked through, adding more water if needed. Stir in cream; return to a fast simmer. Serves 6 to 8.

Host a neighborhood spruce-up! Everyone can help trim bushes and pull bloomed-out annuals...even kids can rake leaves. End with a simple supper for all.

Market Basket Sides & Salads

Grandma Boo's Corn Salad

Jill Daghfal
Plano, IL

My Grandma Beulah was an incredible cook and we all grew up eating this delicious salad at her house. She is 96 now and is no longer able to cook, but I make it for my own family and it's one of our favorites!

15-oz. can white shoepeg corn, drained
14-1/2 oz. can cut green beans, drained

15-oz. can petite peas, drained
1 onion, diced
1 green pepper, diced
1 small red pepper, diced

Mix together all ingredients in a large bowl. Drizzle with Dressing; mix well. Cover and refrigerate until serving time. Serves 8.

Dressing:

3/4 c. vinegar
1 c. sugar
1/4 c. oil

1 T. water
1 t. salt
1/4 t. pepper

Mix together all ingredients in a saucepan over medium-low heat. Cook and stir until sugar dissolves; do not boil. Cool to room temperature.

On warm fall days, set up harvest tables and chairs outdoors for a potluck supper. Decorate with plump pumpkins, bittersweet wreaths, straw bales and scarecrows.

Market Basket
Sides & Salads

Tangy Broccoli Salad

Teri Lindquist
Gurnee, IL

This salad is so fresh and delicious with just about any meal. I mainly use broccoli, but you can mix it up and use 1/2 broccoli and 1/2 cauliflower. My favorite time of year for this salad is summer and early fall when we barbecue...it is so hearty that I only need to add some bread to go along with the main course.

3 thick slices bacon
3 lbs. broccoli, cut into bite-size flowerets
1 pt. grape tomatoes
1/3 c. extra-virgin olive oil

1/4 c. cider vinegar
3 T. light brown sugar, packed
1 T. Dijon mustard
2 cloves garlic, minced
salt and pepper to taste

Cook bacon in a skillet over medium heat until crisp. Drain on paper towels; crumble bacon when cooled. In a large salad bowl, combine broccoli, tomatoes and crumbled bacon. In a small bowl, whisk together remaining ingredients. Pour over vegetables and toss. Cover and refrigerate at least one to 2 hours before serving, stirring occasionally. Broccoli will shrink as it is refrigerated. Makes 6 to 8 servings.

As autumn evenings turn dark, light a candle or two at the family dinner table. It'll make an ordinary meal seem special!

Autumn Recipes
from the Farmhouse

Deviled Potato Salad

Linda Rich
Bean Station, TN

A friend gave me this recipe many years ago. It is wonderful!
I have served to my family several times.

6 potatoes, peeled and cooked
8 eggs, hard-boiled, peeled
   and halved
2 T. vinegar
1 T. prepared horseradish,
   or more to taste
2-1/2 t. mustard
1 c. mayonnaise

1 c. sour cream
1/2 t. celery salt
1 t. salt
1 c. celery, chopped
1/4 c. onion, chopped
2 T. green pepper, chopped
2 T. diced pimentos

Cube potatoes; set aside in a large bowl. Remove egg yolks to a bowl; mash yolks and blend with vinegar, horseradish and mustard. Add mayonnaise, sour cream and salts; mix well and set aside. Chop egg whites and add to potatoes, along with celery, onion, green pepper and pimentos. Fold in egg yolk mixture. Cover and chill until serving time. Makes 10 servings.

Autumn weather can be so fickle, chilly one moment, then balmy the next...so keep some apple cider on hand. Whether it's served chilled or piping-hot, it's always refreshing.

Garden State Tomato & Corn Salad

*Michelle Papp
Rutherford, NJ*

With an abundance of fresh produce here in our state of New Jersey, we always have plenty of locally grown vegetables to enjoy. This makes a great side dish with grilled steak, chicken or pork.

6 ears sweet corn, husks
    removed
2 to 3 tomatoes, chopped
1/2 c. cucumber, chopped
1/2 c. red pepper, chopped
1 red onion, finely chopped

8-oz. pkg. fresh mozzarella
    cheese pearls, drained
6 fresh basil leaves, chopped
salt and pepper to taste
raspberry-walnut vinaigrette
    salad dressing to taste

Add ears of corn to a large pot of boiling water. Cook over high heat for 10 minutes; drain. Cool; cut corn from cobs with a sharp knife. In a large bowl, combine corn with remaining vegetables, cheese and basil. Mix gently; season with salt and pepper. Add salad dressing to taste; mix well. Cover and chill. Serves 6 to 8.

Before the first frost, pick any green tomatoes left in the garden. Wrap each in newspaper and store in a box at room temperature. They'll ripen over the next few weeks, for one last taste of summer.

Autumn Recipes
from the Farmhouse

Apples & Romaine Salad

Gail Blain
Grand Island, NE

*During apple season, we eat lots of apples! This salad
is one of my favorites.*

2 c. Granny Smith apples, cored
   and chopped
2 c. Braeburn apples, cored
   and chopped
1/4 c. crumbled blue cheese

2 slices bacon, cooked and
   crumbled
4 c. mixed salad greens or crisp
   romaine hearts

Combine apples, cheese and bacon in a bowl. Drizzle with Dressing; toss
gently to coat. To serve, arrange greens on salad plates. Spoon apple
mixture over greens. Serves 6.

Dressing:

1/4 c. lemon juice
2 T. honey
1 t. olive oil

1/8 t. salt
1/8 t. pepper

Combine all ingredients in a small bowl; stir well with a whisk.

For nifty placecard holders, simply make a small slice in
colorful gourds or mini pumpkins. Write guests' names
on cards and tuck into the slits.

Market Basket Sides & Salads

Overnight Spinach Salad

Karen Wilson
Defiance, OH

*This is a delicious salad. It's easily made ahead,
so you have more time to spend with your guests.*

1 lb. fresh spinach, torn into
bite-size pieces
1 bunch red leaf lettuce, torn
into bite-size pieces
10-oz. pkg. frozen peas, thawed
2 eggs, hard-boiled, peeled and
chopped

6 slices bacon, crisply cooked
and crumbled
8-oz. container sour cream
1 c. mayonnaise
1.8-oz. pkg. Italian salad
dressing mix

Layer spinach and lettuce in a large salad bowl. Top with peas, eggs
and bacon; set aside. In another bowl, stir together sour cream,
mayonnaise and salad dressing mix; spread over top of salad. Cover
and refrigerate at least 8 hours. Makes 8 servings.

Mix up some herb vinegar. Fill a canning jar with a cup of finely
chopped fresh herbs like parsley, chives and dill. Heat 2 cups white
wine vinegar just to boiling and add to jar. Cap the jar and let steep,
shaking it gently now and then. After 3 weeks, strain the vinegar...
use it to jazz up salads and deli sandwiches.

Autumn Recipes
from the Farmhouse

Chilled Rainbow Pasta Salad

Nancy Kaiser
York, SC

This salad is fairly quick & easy to make and very tasty. Whenever I take it somewhere, someone is sure to ask for the recipe!

16-oz. pkg. rainbow radiatore
    pasta, uncooked
4 green onions, chopped
1 green pepper, chopped
4 stalks celery, diced

2/3 c. sugar
1/2 c. canola oil
1/3 c. catsup
1/4 c. white wine vinegar
1 t. salt

Cook pasta according to package directions; drain. Rinse with cold water; drain again. Mix pasta and vegetables in a large bowl; set aside. Combine remaining ingredients in a small bowl, stirring until sugar is dissolved. Pour over pasta mixture, tossing to coat evenly. Cover and refrigerate until ready to serve. Serves 8 to 10.

24-Hour Slaw

Marlene Burns
Swisher, IA

This tasty coleslaw goes with all kinds of meals...just mix it up ahead of time and tuck it in the fridge.

1 head cabbage, shredded
1 sweet onion, grated
1 green pepper, grated
1-1/2 c. sugar

1/2 c. white vinegar
2 t. salt
1 t. celery seed
1 t. mustard seed

Combine cabbage, onion and green pepper in a bowl; toss to mix. In a small bowl, combine remaining ingredients; mix well and pour over cabbage mixture. Cover and refrigerate overnight before serving. Will keep for several weeks. Makes 8 to 10 servings.

Wrap glass votives with autumn leaves, secured with strands of raffia. So pretty!

Market Basket Sides & Salads

Chopped Zucchini Salad

Chris Schank
Sandwich, IL

Our family loves this simple, fresh-tasting salad all during the year, especially at Thanksgiving, when it's a nice contrast to the tart cranberry sauce. Serve in a clear glass bowl.

1 bunch romaine lettuce, chopped
15-1/4 oz. can corn, drained and rinsed
15-oz. can garbanzo beans, drained and rinsed

2 to 3 zucchini, diced
1/4 c. red onion, thinly sliced
juice of 2 lemons
1/2 c. olive oil
1/2 c. shredded Parmesan cheese

Combine lettuce and all vegetables in a large bowl; set aside. In a small bowl, whisk together lemon juice and olive oil; drizzle over salad and toss to mix well. Sprinkle with Parmesan cheese. Cover and refrigerate until serving time. Makes 6 to 8 servings.

Take in a small-town parade for real hometown spirit. Marching bands, horse-drawn wagons and antique cars...what fun! Remember to take along a blanket to sit on, some trail mix for munching and some mini flags for the kids to wave.

Autumn Recipes from the Farmhouse

Green & White Tossed Pear Salad

Eileen Bennett
Jenison, MI

So quick & easy to prepare, and so pretty! My family loves to cook and eat, and we try to outdo each other with new recipes. When I first tried this recipe, I loved the color combination of fresh greens, sliced pears and toasted pecans. Everyone else raved about the taste!

1 c. chopped pecans
19-oz. pkg. romaine lettuce salad mix

9-oz. pkg. baby spinach
2 Bartlett pears, cored and thinly sliced

Make Buttermilk Dressing a day ahead; refrigerate. Spread pecans in a single layer on an ungreased shallow baking sheet. Bake at 350 degrees for 5 to 6 minutes, stirring once or twice, until lightly golden, toasted and fragrant. Let cool. To assemble, toss romaine lettuce, spinach, pears and pecans in a large bowl; mix gently. Serve with dressing on the side. Makes 8 to 10 servings.

Buttermilk Dressing:

1/2 c. buttermilk
1/2 c. sour cream
1/4 c. grated Parmesan cheese
1 clove garlic, minced

1 t. sugar
1 t. coarse pepper
1/2 t. kosher salt

Whisk together all ingredients. Cover and chill overnight.

Keep tailgating food cold...fill plastic bottles with homemade lemonade or iced tea, freeze and tuck into your picnic cooler. They'll thaw by mealtime.

Market Basket
Sides & Salads

Greek Penne Pasta Salad

Glenda VanEvery
Wixom, MI

Whenever I make this salad for a family get-together or birthday there isn't much left! It's a great salad for picnics, tailgating or just a quick & easy side anytime.

2 16-oz. pkgs. penne pasta, uncooked
1 green pepper, sliced into thin strips
1 red pepper, sliced into thin strips
1 red onion, quartered and sliced into thin strips
1 pt. grape tomatoes, quartered
2 3.8-oz. cans sliced black olives, well drained
4 4-oz. containers crumbled feta cheese
2 16-oz. bottles Greek vinaigrette salad dressing

Cook pasta according to package directions; drain. Rinse with cold water; drain well and place in a large bowl. Add peppers, onion, tomatoes, olives and cheese; mix well. Drizzle with dressing, one bottle at a time. (Second bottle may not be needed, but the pasta does absorb the dressing.) Cover and chill until ready to serve. Before serving, mix salad again, adding more dressing if needed. Serves 12.

Create a fall centerpiece in a snap! Hot-glue ears of multicolored mini Indian corn around a terra-cotta pot and set a vase of yellow mums in the center.

Autumn Recipes from the Farmhouse

Apple-Pear Sauce

Donna Carter
Ontario, Canada

Family & friends love this recipe. It's very tasty...so easy using the slow cooker! Great with roast pork or baked ham, or spooned over ice cream or frozen yogurt. Yummy!

2 lbs. Jonagold apples, peeled, cored and chopped
2 lbs. Anjou pears, peeled, cored and chopped
3/4 c. water
1/4 c. sugar
1/4 c. brown sugar, packed
1 T. lemon juice
4-inch cinnamon stick
1/8 t. salt
Optional: cinnamon to taste

Spray a 5-quart slow cooker with non-stick vegetable spray. Add all ingredients except optional cinnamon. Cover and cook on low setting for 4-1/2 to 5-1/2 hours, until fruit is softened. Crush fruit with a potato masher to desired consistency, either smooth or chunky. Discard cinnamon stick. Serve sauce warm or cold, sprinkled with cinnamon, if desired. Keep refrigerated or frozen. Makes 6 cups.

Store brown sugar in an airtight container to keep it soft.
Too late? For a quick fix, place dried-out brown sugar in a
microwave-safe bowl and cover first with a damp paper towel,
then plastic wrap. Microwave on high for 30 seconds to
one minute, fluff with a fork and use immediately.

Waldorf Salad

Nan Wysock
New Port Richey, FL

I started making this while I was a child and my family has always loved it. It is so much better than versions with sweetened mayonnaise dressings.

5 eggs, beaten
1-1/3 c. sugar
1-1/3 c. pineapple juice
1/2 c. orange juice
1/3 c. lemon juice
1/8 to 1/4 t. salt

1 to 2 c. whipping cream
5 to 6 apples, cored and cut into
    1/2-inch cubes
2 c. seedless red grapes, halved
1 c. pecan pieces
3 stalks celery, diced

In a saucepan, combine eggs, sugar, fruit juices and salt. Cook over low heat, stirring constantly, until thickened. Transfer mixture to a large bowl; set aside to cool completely. With an electric mixer on medium to high speed, beat cream until stiff peaks form. Add whipped cream to egg mixture along with remaining ingredients; stir well. May be served chilled, or frozen in a shallow pan and served in slices. Makes 12 servings.

Candied pecans or walnuts make a salad special. Whisk one egg white with one teaspoon cold water; add a pound of nuts and toss well. Mix one cup sugar, one teaspoon cinnamon and 1/2 teaspoon salt; toss with nuts and spread on a greased baking sheet. Bake at 225 degrees for one hour, stirring once or twice. Store in an airtight container.

Cranberry Pretzel Salad

Ronda Sierra
Woodstock, GA

Our Thanksgiving meal would not be complete without this yummy side dish...or is it a dessert? Whatever you call it, it's scrumptious!

2 c. boiling water
6-oz. pkg. black cherry
  gelatin mix
2 15-oz. cans whole-berry
  cranberry sauce
2 c. pretzel twists, finely crushed

3/4 c. butter, melted
1/2 c. plus 1 T. sugar, divided
8-oz. pkg. cream cheese,
  softened
8-oz. container frozen whipped
  topping, thawed

In a bowl, stir together boiling water and gelatin mix for 2 minutes, or until dissolved. Stir in cranberry sauce. Cover and refrigerate until cooled and partially set. Meanwhile, in a separate bowl, mix together crushed pretzels, melted butter and one tablespoon sugar. Press into the bottom of an ungreased 13"x9" glass baking pan. Bake at 350 degrees for 8 minutes; set aside to cool. In another bowl, blend together cream cheese, whipped topping and remaining sugar; spread over cooled crust. Spoon cooled gelatin over cream cheese mixture. Cover and refrigerate overnight, or until set. Cut into squares. Serves 12.

Fruity gelatin salads are yummy topped with a dollop of creamy lemon mayonnaise. Combine 1/2 cup mayonnaise and 3 tablespoons each of lemon juice, light cream and powdered sugar. Garnish with a sprinkle of lemon zest, if desired.

Kathy's Holiday Cranberry Sauce

Kathy Harrison
Hereford, TX

I've been on the hunt for the perfect cranberry sauce that would please both young and old. I grew up eating the jellied stuff from the can, which I still love! However, I wanted a more flavorful and interesting cranberry sauce. Over several years and many, many tweaks, trials and errors, I finally landed on a recipe that my family adores. I hope you and your family will too!

12-oz. pkg. fresh cranberries
1 c. water
1 c. brown sugar, packed
1/2 t. cinnamon
1/2 t. ground allspice
1/4 t. ground cloves
1/4 t. ground ginger
15-1/4 oz. can pineapple tidbits, drained
Optional: 3/4 to 1 c. walnut or pecan pieces

Combine cranberries, water, brown sugar and spices in a saucepan. Bring to a boil over medium heat; boil until cranberries begin to pop. Reduce heat to a simmer. Continue to cook, stirring often, until berries are popped and mixture is thickened. Remove from heat; stir in pineapple tidbits and nuts, if using. Serve warm, or cover and chill. Makes 6 to 8 servings.

Why, it's the climax of the year,
The highest time of living!
Till naturally its bursting cheer
Just melts into Thanksgiving.
–Paul Lawrence Dunbar

Autumn Recipes *from the Farmhouse*

Sara's Marinated Vegetables

Sara Voges
Washington, IN

An easy, delicious recipe that's perfect for school potlucks and tailgating picnics. Keep it in the fridge to liven up everyday meals, too!

1 large bunch broccoli, cut into
  bite-size flowerets
1 head cauliflower, cut into
  bite-size flowerets
12-oz. pkg. crinkle-cut carrot
  chips
1 green, red or yellow pepper,
  cut into bite-size pieces

1 red onion, cut into bite-size
  pieces
1 c. canola oil
1 c. Italian salad dressing
1 c. red wine vinegar
1 c. sugar
1 T. dried oregano

Combine all vegetables in a large bowl; set aside. In another bowl, whisk together remaining ingredients; pour over vegetables and toss to coat. Cover and refrigerate for 2 hours. Stir again just before serving. Makes 8 servings.

Roasted Brussels Sprouts

LaDeana Cooper
Batavia, OH

*To my family, nothing says fall like fresh Brussels sprouts...
the kids love them!*

2 lbs. Brussels sprouts, trimmed
1 to 2 T. olive oil
2 to 3 cloves garlic, minced

salt and pepper to taste
Optional: grated Parmesan
  cheese

Cut small sprouts in half; cut larger sprouts into quarters. Place sprouts in a bowl. Add oil and garlic; toss to coat. Spread evenly on a parchment paper-lined rimmed baking sheet; season with salt and pepper. Broil for 15 to 20 minutes, until fork-tender, stirring halfway through. Remove from oven. Top with Parmesan cheese, if desired. Serves 6.

Market Basket Sides & Salads

Fresh Garden Vegetable Sauté

Linda Jones
Dry Ridge, KY

*My sister Lila shared this with me over 20 years ago.
Both ways are so good!*

2 T. oil
2 zucchini, sliced
1 yellow squash, sliced
3/4 c. sweet onion, chopped

Optional: minced garlic to taste
3 tomatoes, diced
2 ears corn, kernels cut off
salt and pepper to taste

Heat oil in a skillet over medium heat; add zucchini, yellow squash, onion and minced garlic, if using. Sauté for about 5 minutes. Add tomatoes and corn; season with salt and pepper. Sauté over medium heat for 20 minutes, until all vegetables are tender and well blended. Makes 4 servings.

Variation: Sauté vegetables as directed, then spoon them into a lightly greased 13"x9" baking pan. Cover with shredded Cheddar cheese; crumble buttery round crackers over all. Cover and bake at 350 degrees for 30 minutes, or until bubbly and cheese is melted.

A tried & true kid craft...leaf art! Send out the kids to find colorful leaves, then press the leaves in a heavy book between pieces of wax paper for a few days. Glue leaves to colored paper to form a picture. Twigs, seed pods and acorn caps can be added too. Finish by drawing on details.

Autumn Recipes
from the *Farmhouse*

Caramelized Sweet Potato Wedges

Rosemary Lightbown
Wakefield, RI

My family enjoys this recipe every Thanksgiving...it's a
tasty change from the usual sweet potato casserole.

5 T. butter, divided
4 to 5 sweet potatoes, peeled and
    cut into 1/2-inch wedges
1/4 c. water
3/4 c. brown sugar, packed

1-1/2 t. cinnamon
1/2 t. nutmeg
1/8 t. ground ginger
1 t. salt

Coat a 13"x9" baking pan with one tablespoon butter; set aside. Put
sweet potatoes in a large bowl; set aside. In a saucepan, melt remaining
butter over medium heat. Add water, brown sugar, spices and salt. Cook
and stir until sugar is dissolved. Pour mixture over sweet potatoes; toss
to coat well and spread evenly in pan. Cover and bake at 400 degrees
for about 45 minutes, until tender. Increase oven temperature to
475 degrees. Uncover and spoon sugar mixture in pan over potatoes.
Bake, uncovered, another 15 to 20 minutes, until syrup is thickened
and caramelized. Makes 8 to 10 servings.

Set a packet of pumpkin seeds at each place setting for a fun,
colorful favor...check end-of-season sales for bargains.
Guests can save them to plant in next year's garden.

Cheesy Mashed Potatoes

Lanita Anderson
Lake Lure, NC

I found this recipe many years ago on a carton of sour cream. I was a newlywed and looking for new recipes, so I decided to give it a try! Over the years, I've cooked it for my family, shared it with friends and taken it to potlucks. It has that homemade comfort food feel.

8 baking potatoes, peeled and
   cut into chunks
1/4 c. butter, softened
1/2 t. salt
1/2 t. pepper
8-oz. pkg. shredded Cheddar
   cheese
8-oz. container sour cream
3 T. green onions, sliced
Garnish: paprika to taste

Cover potatoes with water in a saucepan. Boil over high heat until tender, about 15 minutes. Drain; add butter, salt and pepper. Mash potatoes, leaving a few chunks. Add cheese, sour cream and green onions; mix well. Spoon into a greased 3-quart casserole dish. Bake, uncovered, at 350 degrees for 25 to 30 minutes. Just before serving, sprinkle with paprika. Makes 8 servings.

Pray for peace and grace and spiritual food;
for wisdom and guidance, for all these are good,
but don't forget the potatoes!

–John Tyler Pette

Autumn Recipes from the *Farmhouse*

Rice Spice

Janis Parr
Ontario, Canada

This rice dish with all the spices reminds me of holiday stuffing.
Delicious! Be prepared to share the recipe.

3 T. butter
2 c. long-grain white rice,
   uncooked
2/3 c. onion, chopped
1/2 t. salt
2 c. beef consommé

2-1/2 c. water
1.35-oz. pkg. onion soup mix
1/2 t. dried marjoram
1/2 t. dried thyme
1/2 t. dried basil
1/2 t. dried sage

Melt butter in a skillet over medium heat; add rice and onion. Season with salt; sauté until rice is lightly golden. Spoon rice mixture into a lightly greased 2-quart casserole dish. Add remaining ingredients; stir well to combine. Cover top tightly with aluminum foil and a lid. Bake at 375 degrees for one hour; do not uncover while baking. Fluff rice with a fork. Makes 10 servings.

Roasted Parmesan Potatoes

Julie Dossantos
Fort Pierce, FL

With two kinds of potatoes! This is a wonderful easy
side dish that tastes great in the autumn months.
Pairs well with roast beef or chicken.

3 russet potatoes, sliced
   1/2-inch thick
3 sweet potatoes, sliced
   1/2-inch thick

2 T. olive oil
salt and pepper to taste
2 T. grated Parmesan cheese

Layer potatoes in a greased 13"x9" glass baking pan, alternating between russet and sweet, in rows running lengthwise. (Imagine dominoes as they fall.) Drizzle with olive oil; season with salt and pepper. Bake, uncovered, at 375 degrees for 25 minutes. Sprinkle with cheese; increase heat to 400 degrees. Bake for an additional 10 to 15 minutes, until cooked through and lightly golden. Makes 4 to 6 servings.

Market Basket
Sides & Salads

Old-Fashioned Turkey Dressing

Carolyn Keenan
Gibson Island, MD

My grandmother and mother always made this
simple dressing whenever they roasted a turkey.

1 lb. ground pork sausage
1 c. onion, chopped
2 stalks celery, diced
2 c. chicken broth

1 loaf sliced white bread, cubed
chopped fresh parsley to taste
salt and pepper to taste
2 eggs, beaten

Brown sausage, onion and celery in a skillet over medium heat. Drain; add chicken broth, cubed bread, parsley, salt and pepper. Blend in eggs. Spoon mixture into a greased 3-quart casserole dish. Bake, uncovered, at 350 degrees for 45 minutes, or until heated through and set. Makes 8 to 10 servings.

Gravy is a must with mashed potatoes and dressing! Measure 1/4 cup pan drippings into a skillet over medium heat. Stir in 1/4 cup flour; cook and stir until smooth and bubbly. Add 2 cups skimmed pan juices or broth; cook and stir until boiling. Boil for about one minute, to desired thickness. Season with salt and pepper and serve.

Autumn Recipes from the Farmhouse

Baked Macaroni & Cheese

Michele Shenk
Manheim, PA

I've been making this recipe for years for my family, served with a side of stewed tomatoes! When I take this to a potluck or a family gathering, they always ask, "What kind of cheese do you use?"

16-oz. pkg. elbow macaroni,
  uncooked
1/4 c. cornstarch
2 t. salt
1/2 t. pepper

1 t. dry mustard
5 c. 2% milk
1/4 c. margarine
16-oz. pkg. pasteurized process
  cheese, cubed and divided

Cook macaroni according to package directions, just until tender; drain. Meanwhile, combine cornstarch, salt, pepper and mustard in a large saucepan over medium heat. Stir in milk until smooth. Add margarine; cook and stir constantly, bringing mixture to a boil. Cook and stir for one minute longer; remove from heat. Set aside 1/2 cup of cheese for topping. Stir in remaining cheese until melted. Add cooked macaroni to cheese mixture. Transfer to a greased 13"x9" baking pan; sprinkle with reserved cheese; mix well. Bake, uncovered, at 375 degrees for about 30 minutes, until hot and bubbly. Makes 10 to 12 servings.

Pick any late-blooming herbs in the garden and tuck the stems into a grapevine wreath. They'll dry naturally, keeping their sweet and spicy scents.

Market Basket Sides & Salads

Roasted Parmesan Green Beans

Ann Tober
Biscoe, AR

Whenever a neighbor shares their bounty from the garden, I try to return the favor by making something for them from their garden. You would be surprised to see what shows up on my doorstep!

1 lb. fresh green beans, trimmed
2 T. olive oil
2 T. grated or shredded
   Parmesan cheese

2 T. panko bread crumbs
1/4 t. garlic powder
1/2 t. salt
1/2 t. pepper

Combine all ingredients in a large bowl; toss to coat. Spread green beans on an ungreased large rimmed baking sheet. Bake at 400 degrees for 15 to 20 minutes, stirring halfway through. Serves 4.

Judy's Corn Pudding

Judy Monahan
Waverly, VA

This recipe is a family favorite. They all love my corn pudding! I use corn grown on our farm that I have frozen over the summer.

2 c. fresh or frozen corn
3 eggs, beaten
2-1/4 c. milk
1/3 c. sugar

2 T. all-purpose flour
1-1/2 T. butter, melted
1 t. vanilla extract
1/8 t. salt

Mix corn and eggs in a bowl; set aside. In another bowl, stir together remaining ingredients. Add corn mixture; stir well and pour into a greased 2-quart casserole dish. Set in a shallow pan of hot water. Bake, uncovered, at 350 degrees for one hour, or until firm. Serves 10 to 12.

If you love fresh cranberries, stock up in the fall and freeze unopened bags. You'll be able to add their fruity tang to recipes year 'round.

Autumn Recipes from the Farmhouse

Butternut Squash Bake

Marsha Baker
Pioneer, OH

Everyone loves this dish. I am asked to bring it to church potlucks, and one of my friends loves to call out, "Marsha's squash is here!" When I've served it to company, they said they didn't need dessert, they would just eat more squash. I like to double the topping ingredients for extra deliciousness.

2 c. butternut squash, cubed
   and cooked
1/3 c. butter, softened
2/3 c. sugar

2 eggs, beaten
5-oz. can evaporated milk
1 t. vanilla extract

Mash squash in a bowl; set aside. In a large bowl, beat butter and sugar with an electric mixer on medium speed. Beat in eggs, evaporated milk and vanilla. Stir in squash; mixture will be thin. Spoon mixture into a greased 11"x7" baking pan. Bake, uncovered, at 350 degrees for 45 minutes, or until almost set. Remove from oven and sprinkle with Topping. Bake another for 8 to 10 minutes, until bubbly. Makes 6 to 8 servings.

Topping:

1/2 c. crispy rice cereal, crushed
1/4 c. brown sugar, packed

1/4 c. chopped pecans
2 T. butter, melted

Combine all ingredients in a bowl; mix well.

In late October or early November, plant flowering bulbs for springtime color...it's the ideal time! You'll find lots of daffodil and tulip bulbs in garden centers.

Bacon Bean Pot

Regina Vining
Warwick, RI

*We love the robust flavor of these slow-cooker beans. They're
delicious alongside grilled meats...perfect for tailgating!
Mix & match the beans as you like.*

1/2 lb. bacon, chopped
1 c. onion, chopped
1 c. favorite barbecue sauce
3/4 c. regular or non-alcoholic
   dark beer
1/4 c. brown sugar, packed

2 15-1/2 oz. cans pinto beans,
   drained
2 15-1/2 oz. cans black beans,
   drained
15-1/2 oz. can cannellini beans,
   drained

In a large skillet over medium heat, cook bacon and onion until bacon
is crisp; drain and transfer mixture to a lightly greased 4-quart slow
cooker. Add remaining ingredients; mix well. Cover and cook on low
setting for 4 to 6 hours, until hot and bubbly. Stir again just before
serving. Makes 24 servings.

Invite friends to spend an evening around the fire pit. A simple
meal of roasted hot dogs and baked beans is perfect. As the
fire burns down, it's time to tell ghost stories (not too scary,
if little kids are present) and admire the stars in the clear
night sky. Ahhh...autumn!

Autumn Recipes from the Farmhouse

Pat's Cranberry Chutney

Pat Martin
Riverside, CA

I've served this special dish for ten years now, and even those who say they don't like cranberries will eat this! It is easy to prepare ahead of time and keeps well. Its beautiful deep red color works well for Thanksgiving or Christmas or anytime. A great make-ahead for holiday dinners...delicious afterwards on turkey or ham sandwiches!

16-oz. pkg. fresh cranberries
2 c. sugar
1 c. water
1 c. orange juice
1 c. celery, chopped

1 c. golden or dark raisins
1 c. chopped walnuts
1 apple, cored and chopped
1 T. orange zest
1 t. ground ginger

About 2 hours before serving, or up to one week ahead: In a large saucepan over medium heat, combine cranberries, sugar and water. Bring to a boil over medium-high heat, stirring often. Reduce heat to low; simmer for 15 minutes. Remove from heat; stir in remaining ingredients. Cover and refrigerate. Keeps well for at least a week. Makes about 7 cups.

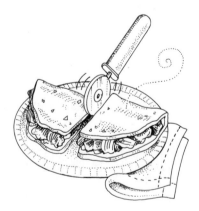

Tired of turkey sandwiches after Thanksgiving? Try a turkey quesadilla! Sprinkle a flour tortilla with chopped turkey, shredded cheese and any other add-ins you like. Top with another tortilla and cook in a lightly greased skillet until cheese melts, turning once. Cut into wedges and serve with salsa. Delicious!

Market Basket
Sides & Salads

Red Cabbage & Apples

Stefanie Murray
Harwich, MA

This is a favorite side dish, especially around Oktoberfest! Served with pork or chicken, it's a delightful side dish to any meal.

3 T. canola oil
1 head cabbage, shredded
2 apples, peeled, cored and cubed
3/4 c. water
1/4 c. sugar
1/2 t. salt
1/4 t. pepper
1/8 t. ground cloves
1/4 c. white wine vinegar

Heat canola oil in a large saucepan over medium heat. Add cabbage; cook and stir for 2 to 3 minutes. Stir in apples, water, sugar, salt, pepper and cloves; bring to a boil. Reduce heat to low. Cover and simmer for 30 to 35 minutes, until cabbage is tender. Stir in vinegar; simmer for another 5 minutes. Serves 6.

Curried Apples

Rocki Roccatani
Ontario, CA

This recipe was a real find! For the best flavor, use four to five different types of apples. Yummy!

10 to 12 apples, peeled, cored
    and thinly sliced
1 c. sugar
2 t. curry powder
1-1/2 c. chopped walnuts
    or pecans
6 T. butter, melted

Arrange apples in a lightly greased 13"x9" baking pan. Combine sugar and curry powder; sprinkle over apples and mix thoroughly. Add nuts; mix again. Drizzle with butter. Cover with aluminum foil. Bake at 350 degrees for 45 minutes to one hour, until apples are tender. Makes 10 to 12 servings.

Vintage divided serving dishes are just right for serving up lots of sides without crowding the table.

Autumn Recipes from the Farmhouse

Peggy's Squash Quiche

Joyce Roebuck
Jacksonville, TX

This recipe was given to me by my sister Peggy, who has since passed away. I always think of her when I make this. I've shared the recipe with many people...I hope you'll enjoy it too!

8-1/2 oz. pkg. yellow
   cornbread mix
1 c. shredded Cheddar cheese
3 eggs, lightly beaten
1/2 c. oil
salt and pepper to taste
1-1/2 c. zucchini, thinly sliced

1-1/2 c. yellow squash,
   thinly sliced
1/2 c. onion, sliced, or 1 bunch
   green onions, chopped
Optional: 1/8 t. cayenne pepper,
   diced pimentos, chopped
   green chiles

Combine all ingredients in a bowl; mix well. Spoon into a greased 10" pie plate. Bake, uncovered, at 350 degrees for 45 minutes. Cut into wedges. Serves 8 to 10.

Favorite Baked Potatoes

Rebecca Beiler
Kinzers, PA

This dish is something we made only once a year, for dinner on the day we harvested the corn. It was always a treat... hope you enjoy it as well!

8 baking potatoes
1/2 c. butter, melted

salt and pepper to taste

Slice potatoes very thinly, but not all the way through. Lay potatoes flat in a buttered 3-quart casserole dish. Drizzle butter over potatoes; sprinkle with seasonings. Bake, uncovered, at 350 degrees for 45 minutes to one hour, until tender. Serves 6 to 8.

Serving sweet potatoes? Add a dash of pumpkin pie spice...delicious!

Autumn Mashed Sweet Potatoes & Apples

Karen Antonides
Gahanna, OH

This is a great autumn recipe...it's wonderful at a Thanksgiving or Christmas table. The addition of applesauce adds a delicious sweetness.

2-1/2 lbs. sweet potatoes
1 c. cinnamon-flavored
  applesauce
2 t. lemon juice
1/4 t. salt

1 apple, peeled if desired, cored
  and finely chopped
1/2 c. crispy dried apple chips,
  coarsely broken

Pierce sweet potatoes in several places with a fork. Arrange on paper towels in the microwave. Cook on high for 15 to 20 minutes, until soft when pierced with a fork. (Or place directly on oven rack and bake at 400 degrees for 45 minutes.) Halve potatoes; scoop out potato pulp and place in a large microwave-safe bowl. Mash potatoes; stir in applesauce, lemon juice and salt. Fold apple into potatoes. Microwave on high for 5 minutes, or until heated through. Spoon into a serving bowl and top with apple chips. To make ahead, microwave or bake potatoes the day before serving; scoop, mash and refrigerate. Reheat to serve. Serves 8.

Start a new Thanksgiving tradition. Instead of snoozing after savoring a big dinner together, lead everyone on a brisk walk. Enjoy the fresh crisp air and the last fallen leaves or the first snowflakes...you'll be ready to sample all those scrumptious pies afterwards!

Autumn Recipes
from the Farmhouse

Colorful Roasted Vegetables
Liz Plotnick-Snay
Gooseberry Patch

All kinds of winter vegetables are tasty fixed this way.
Choose a favorite or mix 'em up!

1/2 lb. butternut squash, peeled and seeded	1 sweet potato, peeled
1/2 lb. acorn squash, peeled and seeded	2 T. olive oil
3 to 4 carrots, peeled	3/4 t. salt
1 to 2 beets, peeled	1/2 t. pepper
	Optional: minced fresh chives

Cut all vegetables into one-inch cubes; spread evenly on an ungreased 15"x10" jelly-roll pan. Drizzle with oil; sprinkle with seasonings. Toss to coat and spread evenly on pan. Bake at 425 degrees for 25 to 30 minutes, until fork-tender and beginning to brown, turning halfway through. Sprinkle with chives, if desired. Makes 4 to 6 servings.

Lay a blank card on each dinner plate and invite guests of
all ages to write down what they are most thankful for
this year. Bind the cards together with a ribbon to create
a sweet gratitude book.

Market Basket Sides & Salads

Broccoli Casserole

Kathy Courington
Canton, GA

I first sampled this dish at church potluck and have loved it ever since. Easy and delicious.

2 10-oz. pkgs. frozen chopped broccoli, thawed and drained
10-3/4 oz. can cream of mushroom soup
1 c. shredded Cheddar cheese
1 c. mayonnaise
2 eggs, beaten
1 c. cheese crackers, crushed
1 T. butter, melted

In a large bowl, mix together broccoli, soup, cheese, mayonnaise and eggs. Transfer to a lightly greased 2-quart casserole dish. Mix crushed crackers with melted butter; spread over casserole. Bake, uncovered, at 350 degrees for 30 minutes, or until hot and bubbly. Serves 4 to 6.

Sweet Onion Casserole

Barbara White
Thompson, OH

This recipe is easy and quick...and everybody raves about it! I like to use light sour cream.

1/4 c. butter
4 to 6 sweet onions, thinly sliced
1/4 c. light or regular sour cream
1/2 c. buttery round crackers, crushed

Melt butter in a skillet over medium heat. Add onions and cook until translucent. Remove from heat; stir in sour cream. Transfer mixture to a greased 2-quart casserole dish. Sprinkle crushed crackers on top. Bake, uncovered, at 350 degrees for 25 to 30 minutes, until bubbly and lightly golden. Serves 4 to 6.

If it's Thanksgiving now, Christmas can't be far away. Double your favorite festive casseroles and side dishes, and freeze half for Christmas dinner...what a time-saver!

Autumn Recipes from the *Farmhouse*

Turkey & White Bean Salad

Lori Rosenberg
Cleveland, OH

Sometimes the Thanksgiving meal is more about the leftovers!
Serve with warm pita wedges for a scrumptious light meal.

2-1/2 c. roast turkey, shredded
15-1/2 oz. can cannellini beans,
   drained and rinsed

1 c. red onion, chopped
2 7-inch whole-wheat pitas,
   each cut into 8 wedges

Combine turkey, beans and onion in a large bowl. Drizzle with
Mediterranean Dressing and toss well. Serve with pita wedges. Serves 4.

Mediterranean Dressing:

1-1/2 T. red wine vinegar
1-1/2 T. olive oil
3/4 c. crumbled feta cheese
2 T. fresh rosemary, minced

2 cloves garlic, minced
1/2 t. dry mustard
1/2 t. pepper

Mix all ingredients in a small jar or salad dressing cruet.

A vintage wooden salad bowl is a terrific find. To restore its glowing
finish, sand lightly inside and out with fine sandpaper. Rub a little
vegetable oil over the bowl and let stand overnight. In the morning,
wipe off any excess oil...good as new!

Farmhouse Comfort Foods

Autumn Recipes from the Farmhouse

Sharon's Chicken Delight

Sharon Velenosi
Costa Mesa, CA

Super simple! Put this in the oven and forget it until dinnertime. It makes its own delicious gravy.

3 lbs. chicken pieces,
   skin removed
salt and pepper to taste
3 potatoes, peeled and quartered
3 onions, peeled and quartered
4 carrots, peeled and quartered

1 zucchini, cut into chunks
14-1/2 oz. can cut green beans,
   drained and 1/4 of juice
   reserved
10-3/4 oz. can tomato soup

Arrange chicken pieces in a greased large roasting pan; season with salt and pepper. Arrange potatoes, onions and carrots between the chicken pieces; place zucchini on top of chicken and vegetables. Pour reserved juice from green beans into pan. Spoon soup over chicken and vegetables; sprinkle green beans over all. Cover with aluminum foil. Bake at 350 degrees for one hour and 45 minutes, or until chicken juices run clear and vegetables are fork-tender. Serve chicken and vegetables with gravy from pan. Serves 4 to 6.

Greet guests with a whimsical pumpkin tower on the front porch. Arrange pumpkins and squash in graduated sizes in a stack, using skewers to hold them in place. Clever!

Farmhouse Comfort Foods

Great-Gram's Garden Medley

Sandy Coffey
Cincinnati, OH

After buying fresh veggies at the farmers' market, I wanted to use up what I had in the fridge. Now this is a family favorite. When done, you have an amazing medley of fresh veggies and ham. Serve with a side salad and a warm dinner roll...supper is simple.

1 meaty ham bone
4 baking potatoes, peeled
  and quartered

2 lbs. fresh green beans, trimmed
6 ears sweet corn, kernels cut off
salt and pepper to taste

Combine all ingredients in a large soup pot; cover with water. Bring to a boil over high heat; reduce heat to medium-low. Simmer for 4 to 6 hours, stirring occasionally. Cut ham from bone and return to pot. Makes 4 to 6 servings.

Cottage Cheese Muffins

Julie Ann Perkins
Anderson, IN

I love good fresh rolls and muffins...hope you enjoy this recipe!

3 T. butter
1/3 c. sugar
1/2 c. small-curd cottage cheese
1 t. lemon zest

1 egg, beaten
1-3/4 c. biscuit baking mix
1/2 c. milk

In a bowl, beat butter and sugar with an electric mixer on medium speed until blended. Beat in cottage cheese and lemon zest. Add egg; beat well. Stir in baking mix and milk until moistened. Spoon batter into 12 greased muffin cups. Bake at 350 degrees for 20 minutes. Makes one dozen.

Honey butter is delectable melting into warm muffins. Simply blend 2/3 cup honey with 1/2 cup softened butter.

Zucchini-Pepper Penne

*Tina Hogsten
Miamisburg, OH*

*Almost any of your favorite farm-fresh vegetables can be used
in this recipe! For variety, try adding cooked shrimp
in place of the chicken.*

16-oz. pkg. penne pasta,
   uncooked
8-oz. pkg. cream cheese,
   cubed and softened
3 T. canola oil
2 cloves garlic, minced
1/2 lb. asparagus, chopped

2 zucchini, diced
1 green pepper, finely diced
salt and pepper to taste
2 c. cooked chicken, cubed
1/2 c. grated Parmesan cheese
1/4 c. fresh parsley, chopped

Cook pasta according to package directions. Drain, reserving 3/4 cup of pasta water. Return hot pasta to pot; immediately add cream cheese, stirring to melt. Meanwhile, combine oil and garlic in a large skillet over medium heat. Add vegetables; season with salt and pepper. Cook until vegetables are crisp-tender, stirring often. When vegetables are almost done, stir in cooked chicken. Add vegetable mixture to pasta, stirring to combine. Add Parmesan cheese and enough of reserved pasta water to moisten. Gradually add parsley while stirring. Makes 4 to 6 servings.

Purchase a bundle of wheat straw at a craft store. Arrange
a few stalks on each folded napkin for a beautiful yet simple
reminder of a bountiful harvest.

Spaghetti with Herbed Tomatoes & Cheese

Barbara Klein
Newburgh, IN

We love this meatless pasta dish. It has lots of flavor and is wonderful served with a tossed green salad.

8-oz. pkg. spaghetti or angel hair
  pasta, uncooked
1 clove garlic, minced
2 T. canola oil
3 ripe tomatoes, peeled and diced

1 t. dried basil
1/2 t. salt
1 c. shredded mozzarella cheese
1/4 c. grated Parmesan cheese

Cook pasta according to package directions; drain. Meanwhile, in a saucepan over medium-low heat, cook garlic in oil until tender. Stir in tomatoes, basil and salt. Heat through, stirring occasionally. Turn pasta out onto a large platter; spoon tomato mixture over pasta. Sprinkle with cheeses and serve immediately. Serves 6.

Turn hot dog buns into garlic bread sticks in a jiffy. Spread buns with softened butter, sprinkle with garlic salt and broil until toasty...yum!

Autumn Recipes from the Farmhouse

Halloween Dinner in a Pumpkin

Sarah Cameron
Fort Belvoir, VA

I loved making this dinner for Halloween night for my children as they came home from trick-or-treating in their little costumes. It's such a fun and unusual dinner that leaves lasting memories for whoever eats it. Yum!

1 medium pumpkin	salt and pepper to taste
6-oz. pkg. rice pilaf mix, uncooked	1/4 c. Worcestershire sauce
1 lb. ground beef	3 T. fresh parsley, chopped
1 lb. ground pork sausage	1-1/2 t. sugar
1 onion, chopped	3/4 c. shredded mozzarella cheese
4 cloves garlic, minced	3/4 c. whipping cream

Cut out a "lid" on pumpkin. Clean out seeds, scraping gently to leave most of the pulp. Place pumpkin on a lightly greased baking sheet; set aside. Prepare rice mix according to package directions. Meanwhile, brown beef and sausage in a large stockpot over medium heat; drain. Add onion, garlic, salt and pepper; stir well. Add rice, Worcestershire sauce, parsley and sugar; mix well. Stir in cheese. Spoon mixture carefully into pumpkin, packing lightly. Pour cream on top; do not stir. Put lid on the pumpkin. Set baking sheet with pumpkin in oven on lower rack. Bake at 375 degrees for 50 to 90 minutes, until a knife tip can be easily inserted into pumpkin. When serving, be sure to get a spoonful of pumpkin pulp along with the beef mixture. Serves 6.

Heap seasonal produce in a primitive wooden dough bowl for a bountiful country-style centerpiece...shiny red and yellow peppers in summer, acorn squash and gourds in autumn.

Chili-Ghetti

Judy Brown
Sanger, CA

*Delicious and easy to make...we can't get enough! Always
a hit when lots of family & friends come for dinner.*

2 T. margarine
1 lb. ground beef
3/4 c. onion, chopped
1 clove garlic, minced
2 16-oz. cans chili with meat,
  no beans

14-1/2 oz. can crushed tomatoes
8-oz. pkg. spaghetti, uncooked
3 c. shredded Cheddar cheese
8-oz. container sour cream
1/4 c. grated Parmesan cheese

Melt magarine in a large skillet over medium heat. Add beef, onion
and garlic; cook until browned and drain. Stir in chili and tomatoes
with juice. Simmer over medium-low heat for 45 minutes, stirring
occasionally. Meanwhile, cook spaghetti according to package
directions; drain. Remove skillet from heat; stir in Cheddar cheese and
let stand until melted. Fold in sour cream. Add cooked spaghetti to beef
mixture, mixing well. Turn into a buttered 2-quart casserole; top with
Parmesan cheese. Bake, uncovered, at 350 degrees for 45 minutes, or
until hot and bubbly. Serves 10 to 12.

Serve beverages in old-fashioned Mason jars for real country charm.
Setting the jars inside wire drink carriers makes it easy to
tote them from kitchen to harvest table.

Autumn Recipes from the Farmhouse

Sausage & Rice Casserole

Lanita Anderson
Lake Lure, NC

A comforting, hearty recipe that's perfect for the fall and winter months. Mom used to make this recipe when I was growing up, and it's one of the first recipes I made for my husband after we were married. It's easy to make...tasty served with a tossed salad and warm cornbread.

1 lb. smoked pork sausage, sliced
1/2 c. onion, chopped
10-1/2 oz. can diced tomatoes
   with green chiles
10-3/4 oz. can cream of
   celery soup

1-1/4 c. water
1-1/2 c. instant rice, uncooked
15-1/2 oz. can pinto beans or
   red kidney beans

In a large saucepan, combine sausage, onion, tomatoes, soup and water. Bring to a boil over high heat; reduce heat to medium. Stir in rice and beans. Cover and simmer for 5 minutes, or until rice is done. Makes 8 to 10 servings.

Autumn weather can be so unpredictable! Keep the pantry stocked with canned vegetables, hearty soups, rice and pasta, and you'll always be able to put dinner on the table without going out.

Farmhouse Comfort Foods

Mom's Hamburger Gravy

Sherry Sheehan
Evansville, TN

This is comfort food at its best. My mom was a farm girl from West Virginia, and her dishes were all very simple. I love this gravy served over mashed potatoes, and my husband likes his over hot biscuits. Either way, it is delicious. Sometimes I'll add a one-pound package of frozen mixed vegetables while the ground beef is cooking, to add color and yield a few more servings.

1-1/2 lbs. lean ground beef
2 c. water
1 t. salt
1/2 t. pepper

2 c. milk
3/8 c. all-purpose flour
mashed potatoes or hot biscuits

Break up beef and cook in a large skillet over medium heat until browned; drain. Add water, salt and pepper; bring to a boil. In a large shaker cup or jar with a tight-fitting lid, combine milk and flour; shake until smooth. Stir milk mixture into beef mixture. Cook, stirring constantly, until thickened and smooth. Remove from heat. To serve, ladle over mashed potatoes or hot biscuits. Makes 6 servings.

Life starts all over again
when it gets crisp in the fall.
– F. Scott Fitzgerald

Autumn Recipes from the Farmhouse

Herbed Turkey Breast

Tonya Sheppard
Galveston, TX

Topped with buttery pan juices, this turkey is delicious!

4 to 5-lb. turkey breast, thawed
   if frozen
6 T. butter, softened
1 T. fresh parsley, finely chopped
1 T. fresh sage, finely chopped

1 T. fresh thyme, finely chopped
2 t. salt
1/2 t. pepper
1 c. chicken broth

Pat turkey breast dry with paper towels. Gently separate the skin, leaving it attached around the edges. Blend butter, herbs and seasonings in a small bowl; rub butter mixture underneath skin. Place breast in an ungreased shallow roasting pan. Bake, uncovered, at 325 degrees for one hour and 45 minutes to 2 hours, basting several times while baking, until a meat thermometer inserted in thickest part reads 165 degrees. Remove breast to a deep platter; lightly tent with aluminum foil and let stand for 15 minutes. Meanwhile, add chicken broth to juices in roasting pan; scrape up browned bits in the bottom of pan and transfer to a saucepan. Let stand a few minutes; spoon off fat. Bring broth mixture to a boil over high heat; boil until cooked down to 3/4 cup. Slice turkey thinly; ladle broth mixture over turkey. Serves 8.

Thanksgiving dinner is all about tradition! Keep it simple with tried & true recipes everyone loves and looks for...sweet potato casserole, corn pudding and cranberry sauce. Perhaps add just one or two simple new dishes for variety. Then relax and enjoy your guests!

Farmhouse Comfort Foods

Simple Creamed Turkey

Tina Butler
Royse City, TX

*Good old-fashioned comfort food! This is the perfect way
to use up leftover roast turkey from Thanksgiving. Serve with
leftover stuffing and rolls for a complete meal.*

1 c. celery, thinly sliced	3 c. roast turkey, cubed
1/2 c. onion, chopped	1 T. lemon juice
6 T. butter	1/4 t. dried thyme
1/4 c. all-purpose flour	1/2 t. salt
1-1/2 c. chicken broth	pepper to taste
1 c. milk	cooked rice or mashed potatoes

In a large saucepan over medium heat, sauté celery and onion in butter
for 5 minutes, or until crisp-tender. Gradually stir in flour; cook and stir
over low heat until flour is dissolved and mixture is bubbly. Slowly add
chicken broth, stirring constantly. Add milk; bring to a boil and simmer,
stirring often. Stir in turkey, lemon juice and seasonings; heat through.
To serve, spoon turkey mixture over cooked rice or mashed potatoes.
Makes 4 servings.

Thanksgiving is so family-centered...why not have a post-holiday
potluck with friends, the weekend after Turkey Day? Everyone can
bring their favorite "leftovers" concoctions and relax together.

Autumn Recipes
from the Farmhouse

Tuna Noodle Crisp

Faye Mayberry
Benson, AZ

This is a recipe I found in my grandmother's stash of recipes that I've inherited. It's a cheesy little twist on the old classic, tuna noodle casserole. The pimentos give great color!

2 c. wide egg noodles, uncooked
2 t. oil
1/3 c. onion, chopped
2 T. green pepper, chopped
10-3/4 oz. can Cheddar
   cheese soup
1/2 c. milk

1 t. salt
1/8 t. pepper
Optional: 1 T. chopped pimentos,
   drained
6-oz. can tuna, drained and
   flaked
1/2 c. dry bread crumbs

Cook noodles according to package directions; drain. Meanwhile, add oil to a large skillet over medium heat. Add onion and green pepper; cook until tender. Stir in soup, milk, salt, pepper and pimentos, if using; bring to a boil. Fold in cooked noodles and tuna. Transfer mixture to a lightly greased 1-1/2 or 2-quart casserole dish. Sprinkle bread crumbs on top. Bake, uncovered, at 350 degrees for 25 to 30 minutes, until hot and bubbly. Serves 4 to 6.

A family recipe book is a wonderful way to preserve family traditions. Ask everyone to send copies of their most-requested recipes and combine all the recipes into a book. Have copies made for everyone... it's a delightful take-home for Thanksgiving dinner.

Farmhouse Comfort Foods

Chicken with Mushrooms & White Beans

Katie Flaherty
Clinton, MA

One day, I tossed all of these ingredients together in the slow cooker...and now it's one of my favorites.

8-oz. pkg. sliced mushrooms
4 boneless, skinless chicken
   thighs
16-oz. can Great Northern beans
10-3/4 oz. can cream of
   mushroom soup

Layer all ingredients in a 4-quart slow cooker in the order given. Cover and cook on low setting for 6 to 8 hours. Makes 4 servings.

Easy Sweet-and-Sour Chicken

Carrie Kelderman
Pella, IA

This is a handy recipe for a cool fall day...and it smells wonderful when it's done! I can toss it together in the morning & keep in the fridge until late afternoon, then pop it in the oven as I help the kids with homework. It's a favorite for our family! Serve over cooked rice, if desired.

6 chicken breasts, skin removed
10-oz. jar apricot jam
1-oz. pkg. onion soup mix
8-oz. bottle French salad
   dressing

Arrange chicken breasts in a greased 13"x9" baking pan; set aside. In a bowl, stir together jam, soup mix and salad dressing; spoon over chicken. Bake, uncovered, at 350 degrees for one to 1-1/2 hours, occasionally spooning sauce over the chicken as it bakes. Serves 6.

Chicken thighs can be used in most recipes calling for chicken breasts. They're juicier and more flavorful too.

Zucchini & Sausage Casserole *Marjorie Hennig*
Seymour, IN

I had so many zucchini from the garden one year and even some bags of shredded zucchini tucked in the freezer from the previous year. After I'd used zucchini in every conceivable way, I decided to experiment. This casserole is the result...we think it's delicious!

1 lb. sweet Italian ground pork
   sausage, browned and
   drained
8-1/2 oz. pkg. cornbread mix
10-oz. pkg. frozen corn, thawed
3 c. zucchini, shredded
1 onion, finely chopped

2 eggs, beaten
1-1/2 t. garlic, minced
1/2 t. dried dill weed
1/2 t. salt
1-1/4 c. shredded Cheddar
   cheese, divided

Combine sausage and dry cornbread mix in a lightly greased 2-quart casserole dish. Add remaining ingredients, setting aside 1/4 cup cheese for topping. Mix gently. Bake, uncovered, at 350 degrees for about 50 minutes, until a knife tip inserted in the center comes out clean. Top with reserved cheese; return to oven long enough to melt the cheese. Serves 8 to 10.

Invite friends and neighbors over for a backyard festival on a sunny autumn day. Games like cornhole, bobbing for apples, Red Rover and three-legged races add old-fashioned fun!

Farmhouse Comfort Foods

Gram's Pork Chops with Potatoes & Sauerkraut

Judy Henfey
Cibolo, TX

Gram and Mom made this dish often. Great as a quick meal and fancy enough for company. Best served with a green salad, some warm chunky applesauce and a loaf of crusty bread...yum!

2-1/2 lbs. bone-in pork chops
1/2 t. salt, divided
1/2 t. pepper, divided
1 T. oil
4 onions, diced
1 c. celery, thinly sliced
32-oz. jar sauerkraut, drained
1/2 t. garlic powder
6 potatoes, peeled and thinly sliced
1 c. white wine or chicken broth
1/2 c. sugar

Season pork chops with 1/4 teaspoon each salt and pepper. In a large skillet over medium-high, brown pork chops in oil on both sides. Remove pork chops to a plate; set aside. Add onions, celery and sauerkraut to skillet. Sauté for 5 minutes, or until golden; season with garlic powder and remaining salt and pepper. Fold potatoes into sauerkraut mixture; transfer to a lightly greased 13"x9" baking pan. Arrange pork chops on top. Whisk together wine or broth and sugar; pour evenly over top. Cover with aluminum foil and bake at 350 degrees for one hour. Serves 4 to 6.

When pork chops are on the menu, sprinkle a little salt in your cast-iron skillet before adding the oil and the meat. You'll have less spattering and more flavorful pork chops.

Autumn Recipes from the Farmhouse

Roast Chicken & Vegetables

Cindy Neel
Gooseberry Patch

This is a very versatile recipe! If you prefer, use your favorite chicken pieces instead of a whole chicken. Change it up with Yukon Gold potatoes and parsnips. Delicious!

3-1/2 lb. roasting chicken
salt and pepper to taste
1 yellow onion, cut into chunks
3 carrots, peeled and cut into
   chunks
2 stalks celery, cut into chunks

1/2 lb. redskin potatoes, halved
   or quartered
1 clove garlic, halved
1 T. butter, melted
1 lemon, halved
1/2 bunch fresh thyme

Pat chicken dry with paper towels; season all over with salt and pepper. Tie legs together with kitchen string; tuck wings under and set chicken aside. Spread vegetables and garlic in a greased 13"x9" baking pan. Place chicken on top; brush with melted butter. Place lemon halves and thyme inside chicken. Bake, uncovered, at 425 degrees for 50 minutes to one hour, until juices run clear and a meat thermometer inserted into the center of the thigh reads 165 degrees. Loosely tent chicken with aluminum foil; let stand for 15 to 20 minutes. Transfer chicken to a cutting board and carve; serve with vegetables. Serves 6.

A simple trick to add down-home flavor to a roasting chicken... cover it with several thick slices of hickory-smoked country bacon before popping it into the oven.

Farmhouse Comfort Foods

Auntie Irene's Tasty Chicken & Rice

Doreen Knapp
Stanfordville, NY

This is from my aunt's cookbook. I cherish all of her handwritten recipes and I have tried so many of them. They always turn out great! She drew little stars next to the ones she really liked.

10-3/4 oz. can cream of chicken soup
10-3/4 oz. can cream of onion soup
1 c. long-cooking white rice, uncooked
1-1/4 c. water
4 boneless, skinless chicken breasts
1 T. Worcestershire sauce
salt and pepper to taste

In a greased 9"x9" baking pan, combine soups, uncooked rice and water; stir gently. Arrange chicken breasts on top. Brush chicken with Worcestershire sauce; season with salt and pepper. Cover with parchment paper and aluminum foil. Bake at 325 degrees for 2 hours. Check occasionally while it's baking to see if additional liquid is needed. Makes 4 servings.

One-Hour Buttermilk Rolls

Pam Hooley
LaGrange, IN

I got this recipe the first year we were married, 45 years ago. The recipe card is old, yellowed and stained from constant use. It's a reliable standby for delicious dinner rolls or sweet rolls.

2 cakes fresh yeast
1/4 c. warm water, 110 to 115 degrees
3 T. sugar
1/2 c. melted shortening or oil
1-1/2 c. buttermilk
1/2 t. baking soda
2 t. salt
4-1/2 c. all-purpose flour

In a large bowl, dissolve yeast in warm water. Add remaining ingredients; mix well. Let rise for 10 minutes. Shape into 18 rolls; arrange in a greased 13"x9" baking pan and let rise 30 minutes. Bake at 400 degrees for 15 to 20 minutes, until golden. Makes 1-1/2 dozen.

Autumn Recipes from the Farmhouse

Grandma Shaffer's Braised Beef Short Ribs

Marcia Shaffer
Conneaut Lake, PA

My son-in-law Jonathan loves beef ribs. I love to cook for him because he is as precious as my son Richard. Beef short ribs are a little more pricey than pork ribs, but worth the money. After baking for two hours, the meat just slides off the bone!

1-1/4 c. all-purpose flour
salt and pepper to taste
3 lbs. beef short ribs
1 to 2 T. oil
1 onion, thinly sliced

1/4 t. dried thyme
1 T. vinegar
2 T. catsup
1/2 c. water

Add flour to a shallow dish; season generously with salt and pepper. Dredge ribs in seasoned flour. Heat oil in a heavy skillet over medium-high heat. Brown ribs on all sides; remove to a greased 3-quart casserole dish. Add remaining ingredients to skillet drippings. Cook and stir until blended and onion is tender; spoon over ribs. Cover and bake at 325 degrees for about 2 hours, until ribs are tender. Serves 4 to 6.

Need a quick snack for the kids before dinner is served? Hand out little bags of crunchy snacks...just toss together bite-size cereal squares, raisins or dried cranberries and a few chocolate-covered candies.

Farmhouse Comfort Foods

Apricot Drummers

Jill Ball
Highland, UT

For some reason, drumsticks are much more fun to eat than plain old chicken breasts! This is one of my boys' favorites.

12 chicken drumsticks
1 t. salt
1/4 t. pepper
1/4 c. apricot jam

1/4 c. mustard
1/4 c. oil
1 T. brown sugar, packed

Season chicken with salt and pepper; set aside. In a small bowl, stir together remaining ingredients for sauce. Grill chicken, covered, over medium heat for 15 to 20 minutes, occasionally turning and basting with sauce. Cool for 5 minutes before serving. Serves 6, 2 drumsticks each.

Harvest Casserole

Sonya Labbe
Quebec, Canada

This dish is a favorite in my family. It can be served as a side dish or it can be a meatless meal in itself, served with a crusty bread.

1 russet potato, peeled and cut
   into 1/2-inch cubes
1 sweet potato, peeled and cut
   into 1/2-inch cubes
2 carrots, peeled and cut into
   1/2-inch slices
5 T. olive oil, divided

salt and pepper to taste
1 red onion, thinly sliced
   into rings
1 to 2 zucchini, thinly sliced
   crosswise
1/2 c. grated Parmesan cheese

In a 13"x9" baking pan, toss potatoes and carrots in 2 tablespoons olive oil. Season with salt and pepper; toss until coated and spread evenly in pan. Arrange onion rings evenly on top; arrange zucchini over onion. Drizzle with 2 tablespoons oil. Season with salt and pepper. Sprinkle cheese over top; drizzle with remaining oil. Bake, uncovered, at 400 degrees for about 40 minutes, until vegetables are tender and topping is golden. Serves 4 to 6.

Autumn Recipes from the Farmhouse

Chicken & Biscuit Bubble-Up

Jessica Kraus
Delaware, OH

*This one-dish recipe is so simple and great for
a chilly-day family meal or a potluck!*

2 c. cooked chicken, diced
10-3/4 oz. can cream of
   chicken soup
1-1/4 c. sour cream
15-oz. can corn, drained
14-1/2 oz. can cut green beans,
   drained
1 c. shredded Colby Jack cheese

1/2 c. onion, diced
1/4 c. bacon, crisply cooked
   and crumbled
1-1/2 T. ranch salad dressing
   mix
16-oz. tube refrigerated biscuits,
   quartered

In a large bowl, combine all ingredients except biscuits; mix well. Fold
biscuit quarters into chicken mixture. Transfer to a greased 13"x9" baking
pan. Bake, uncovered, at 350 degrees for 25 to 30 minutes, until
golden. Makes 8 servings.

If your church hosts an old-fashioned Election Day dinner,
keep an eye open for sales after the Fourth of July...you'll find
oodles of patriotic cups, napkins, plates, banners, buntings and
flags to use for spirited decorating when Election Day rolls around.

Farmhouse Comfort Foods

Mom's Best Meatloaf

Janie Toney
Burlington, NC

Mom was always asked to bring her meatloaf to church dinners and reunions. It really is delicious! And, it makes two meatloaves, so there's plenty for everyone.

3 lbs. ground beef
1-1/3 c. rolled oats, uncooked
2 eggs, beaten
1 green pepper, diced
1 onion, diced
1/4 c. salt
pepper to taste
2 c. brown sugar, packed
1 c. catsup
1 c. mustard

In a large bowl, mix together beef, oats, eggs, green pepper, onion, salt and pepper. Shape into 2 loaves and place each in an ungreased 9"x5" loaf pan. For sauce, stir together remaining ingredients in a separate bowl until smooth and no lumps remain. Divide sauce evenly between meatloaves. Bake, uncovered, at 400 degrees for one hour. Check after 45 minutes. Let cool for 20 minutes before slicing. Makes 2 meatloaves; each serves 6 to 8.

Often, for the tastiest country cooking, no fancy tools are needed... dig right in and mix that meatloaf with your hands!

Autumn Recipes
from the Farmhouse

Super-Easy Supper Skillet

Sharon Velenosi
Costa Mesa, CA

*This recipe is super-easy...just add everything to the skillet
and forget it. You'll have time to cook some rice or noodles,
set the table and call everyone to dinner.*

2 lbs. ground turkey
2 T. margarine
3/4 c. onion, chopped
1 c. green pepper, chopped
1/2 lb. sliced mushrooms

salt and pepper to taste
1 c. shredded Cheddar cheese
2 14-1/2 oz. cans diced tomatoes
cooked rice or noodles

In a large skillet over medium heat, brown turkey in margarine. Stir in
onion, green pepper and mushrooms; season with salt and pepper. Top
with cheese. Pour tomatoes with juice over all; do not stir. Cover and
bring to a boil. Reduce heat to low; simmer for 20 minutes. Serve over
cooked rice or noodles. Makes 6 to 8 servings.

Jon Ben Getty

A'lisa Johnson
Abilene, KS

*Kansas famous! This is an old-time recipe to feed hungry farmers
at the end of a long day of harvest. Sometimes, instead of all
ground beef, I use half pork and half beef.*

7-oz. pkg. wide egg noodles,
  uncooked
1-1/2 lbs. lean ground beef
1-1/2 c. onions, diced
1 green pepper, diced
10-3/4 oz. can cream of
  mushroom soup

10-3/4 oz. can tomato soup
15-1/4 oz. can peas, drained,
  or 10-oz. pkg. frozen peas
4-oz. chopped pimentos, drained
paprika, salt and pepper to taste
8-oz. pkg. shredded Cheddar
  cheese, divided

Cook noodles according to package directions until almost tender; drain.
Meanwhile, in a large skillet over medium heat, brown beef with onions
and pepper; drain. Mix in remaining ingredients, reserving half of
cheese for topping. Spread mixture in a greased 3-quart casserole dish.
Bake, covered, at 350 degrees for 30 minutes. Uncover; top with
remaining cheese. Bake until lightly golden. Serves 6 to 8.

Farmhouse Comfort Foods

Cranberry-Glazed Baked Ham

Vickie
Gooseberry Patch

My family insists on a baked ham as well as a roast turkey for Thanksgiving dinner. This is a delicious and easy recipe that they all love!

4 to 6-lb. fully cooked
  boneless ham
12-oz. can frozen cranberry juice
  cocktail concentrate, thawed
3 T. Dijon mustard

2 T. brown sugar, packed
2 T. lemon juice
4 t. cornstarch
1/4 t. ground cloves

Place ham on a rack in a shallow roasting pan. If desired, use a paring knife to score fat on top of ham in a diamond pattern, cutting 1/4-inch deep. Bake, uncovered, at 325 degrees for 1-1/4 to 2-1/2 hours, depending on size of ham, until a meat thermometer inserted in the thickest part reads 140 degrees. Meanwhile, combine remaining ingredients in a saucepan over medium heat. Cook and stir until thickened and bubbly. Cook and stir for 2 more minutes. During the final 15 minutes of baking, brush glaze over ham. Remove ham to a platter; let stand for 10 minutes before slicing. Serve any remaining glaze alongside ham. Serves 12 to 16.

Make a fun porch sign for Halloween...stencil a saying like "Best Witches" or "Sit for a Spell" on an old plank.

Spicy Cabbage Casserole

Veronica Rankin
Ontario, Canada

This is a recipe my mom passed down to me. It's great on a cool fall day, served with mashed potatoes. Now that she's gone, every time I make it, it brings back fond memories of what a wonderful cook she was! This is the ideal recipe for those chilly autumn days.

1 lb. lean ground beef	1 c. long-cooking rice, uncooked
14-1/2 oz. can diced tomatoes	1 egg, lightly beaten
10-1/2 oz. can French onion	1/2 c. oil
soup or beef broth	1 T. garlic salt
1 head cabbage, finely chopped	1 T. chili powder
1 c. onion, chopped	1 T. salt
1 green pepper, chopped	1/8 t. cayenne pepper

In a large bowl, mix together uncooked beef, tomatoes with juice and remaining ingredients. Turn into a greased roasting pan. Bake, covered, at 350 degrees for 1-1/2 to 2 hours; do not uncover while baking. Serves 6.

Small-town county fairs, food festivals, craft shows, swap meets...the list goes on & on, so pack up the kids and go for good old-fashioned fun!

Farmhouse Comfort Foods

Baked Chicken & Cheese Pasta
Tina Wright
Atlanta, GA

*This was my Grandma Evelyn's tried & true potluck recipe for years!
My family loves it too...it's a great way to enjoy that leftover turkey.
Use elbow macaroni instead of ditalini, if you prefer.*

3 c. ditalini pasta, uncooked
1/2 c. onion, chopped
1/2 c. celery, chopped
1/3 c. butter
1/3 c. all-purpose flour
2 T. chicken bouillon granules

4-1/2 c. whole milk
1-1/2 c. shredded sharp Cheddar
cheese
3 c. cooked chicken, cubed
2-oz. jar diced pimentos, drained
2.8-oz. can French fried onions

Cook pasta according to package directions; drain. Meanwhile, in a
large saucepan over medium heat, cook onion and celery in butter until
tender. Stir in flour and bouillon; gradually stir in milk. Cook and stir
until bubbly and thickened; remove from heat. Add cheese; stir until
melted. Stir in cooked pasta, chicken and pimentos. Transfer to a greased
13"x9" baking pan. Cover and bake at 350 degrees for 30 minutes, or
until hot and bubbly. Uncover and top with onions; bake another
5 minutes. Let stand 10 minutes before serving. Serves 6 to 8.

While you're raking up fallen leaves, keep an eye out for
short branches of colorful leaves, late-blooming flowers and
interesting bare twigs to arrange in a tall vase. You'll have
a wonderful autumn bouquet in no time at all.

Autumn Recipes from the Farmhouse

Beverly's Barbecue Ribs

Beverly Tierney
Lake Alfred, FL

Everyone raves about the homemade sauce on these ribs! It's always requested for get-togethers and is good on any type of meat. Pre-boiling the ribs gives flavor and helps reduce some of the fat. The meat will fall right off the bone!

4 lbs. pork spareribs
3/4 c. onion, quartered
2 t. salt
1/4 t. pepper

Optional: 12-oz. can regular or
non-alcoholic beer
2 T. smoke-flavored cooking
sauce

Start Barbecue Sauce ahead of time. Cut spareribs into serving-size pieces; set aside. In a large stockpot, combine onion, salt, pepper and beer, if using. Add spareribs; cover with water. Bring to a boil over high heat; reduce heat to medium-low. Simmer for 1-1/2 hours, or until ribs are tender. Drain; remove ribs to a large plate or baking sheet. Sprinkle with smoke-flavored sauce; brush with Barbecue Sauce. Grill or broil ribs until browned as desired. Serves 4.

Barbecue Sauce:

1-1/2 c. cider vinegar
1-1/2 c. brown sugar, packed
1-1/2 c. catsup
3/4 c. chili sauce

3/4 c. Worcestershire sauce
6 T. onion, minced
1-1/4 t. dried, minced garlic

Mix all ingredients in a saucepan. Simmer, uncovered, for one hour or until slightly thickened, stirring occasionally. Pour into a container; cover and refrigerate. Makes about one quart.

Vintage tea towels make fun-to-use oversized napkins...perfect when enjoying messy-but-tasty foods like barbecued ribs and fried chicken!

Farmhouse Comfort Foods

Mushroom Pot Roast

Grace Smith
British Columbia, Canada

My family loves my old stand-by, pot roast with mushroom soup, but I wanted to try something new. Turns out, they liked this recipe even better! Serve with mashed potatoes to enjoy the gravy.

1 c. warm water
1 T. beef soup base
1/2 lb. sliced mushrooms
1 c. onion, coarsely chopped
3 cloves garlic, minced
3-lb. boneless beef chuck roast

1/2 t. pepper
1 T. Worcestershire sauce
1/4 c. butter, cubed
1/3 c. all-purpose flour
1/4 t. salt

In a 5-quart slow cooker, whisk together water and soup base; add mushrooms, onion and garlic. Sprinkle roast with pepper; add to slow cooker. Drizzle roast with Worcestershire sauce. Cover and cook on low setting for 6 to 8 hours, until roast is tender. Remove roast to a serving platter; cover loosely with aluminum foil. Strain cooking juices in slow cooker, reserving vegetables; skim fat. In a large saucepan, melt butter over medium heat. Stir in flour and salt until smooth; gradually whisk in cooking juices. Bring to a boil, stirring constantly; cook and stir for one to 2 minutes, until thickened. Stir in cooked vegetables; serve gravy with roast. Makes 6 to 8 servings.

Shake up your pumpkin display! Pumpkins and winter squashes come in lots of sizes, shapes and colors. Carve into Jack-o'-Lanterns, or simply heap in a wheelbarrow.

Autumn Recipes from the Farmhouse

Braised Pork Chops & Red Cabbage

Julie Harris
Mertztown, PA

There are certain things that just let you know that autumn is in the air. The smell of this dish wafting from my mother's country kitchen has always been a sure sign for me! In early September, she would start sifting through her hearty dinner recipes, and you can bet that this was always one of our first chilly-day autumn dinners!

8 bone-in pork chops	1 c. chicken broth
salt and pepper to taste	2 T. balsamic vinegar
4 T. olive oil, divided	2 T. butter, sliced
4 c. red cabbage, shredded	
9-oz. pkg. frozen spinach, thawed	

Season pork chops on both sides with salt and pepper; set aside. Heat 2 tablespoons olive oil in a large skillet over medium heat. Add cabbage; cook and stir until tender. Stir in spinach. Remove cabbage mixture to a platter; set in a warm 200-degree oven. In the same skillet, heat remaining oil. Working in batches if necessary, brown pork chops on both sides; cook until no longer pink in the center. Arrange pork chops on top of cabbage mixture; return platter to warm oven. Stir drippings in skillet, scraping any browned bits loose from bottom of pan. Add chicken broth and vinegar. Cook, stirring often, until sauce reduces to half. Turn off heat; add butter and stir until smooth. Drizzle some of sauce over pork chops on platter; serve remaining sauce on the side. Serves 4 to 6.

Clean up those casserole dishes with baked-on food spatters. Mix equal amounts of cream of tartar and white vinegar into a paste. Spread onto the dish and let stand for 30 minutes to an hour. Spatters will wash off easily.

Farmhouse Comfort Foods

Ozark Beef Roast

Caroline Timbs
Cord, AR

This roast is my grandmother's recipe. She always said that browning the roast first was the secret to this delicious dish. You will be smelling a wonderful aroma all afternoon as it bakes!

3-lb. beef chuck roast
1 c. all-purpose flour
1/4 c. oil
1/2 c. water

8 to 10 potatoes, peeled
and quartered
2 lbs. carrots, peeled
seasoned salt to taste

Coat roast on both sides with flour. Heat oil in a large heavy skillet over medium-high heat. Add roast to skillet; cook on both sides until crisp and brown. Add water to a deep 13"x9" baking pan. Arrange vegetables in pan; sprinkle with seasoned salt. Place roast on top of vegetables; cover with aluminum foil. Bake at 350 degrees for 4 hours. Uncover; bake another 20 minutes, or until coating on top is crisp and golden. Slice roast; serve with vegetables. Serves 8.

Chive & Sour Cream Biscuits

Jackie Smulski
Lyons, IL

Short on time? These also can be made into drop biscuits by dropping dough in ten scoops onto an ungreased cookie sheet. Bake as directed.

2 c. biscuit baking mix
2/3 c. sour cream
2 T. fresh chives, finely snipped

Garnish: 2 T. milk or melted
butter

In a bowl, stir together biscuit mix, sour cream and chives until a soft dough forms. Place dough on a floured surface; shape into a ball and knead 10 times. Roll dough to 1/2-inch thickness. Cut into 10 rounds with a 2-inch biscuit cutter or drinking glass, dipped into flour. On an ungreased cookie sheet, place rounds 2 inches apart. Bake at 400 degrees for 8 to 10 minutes, until golden. Remove from oven; brush with milk or butter. Makes 10 biscuits.

Deep-Dish String Pie

Janis Parr
Ontario, Canada

This is a longtime family favorite of ours. You can add or substitute your choice of chopped vegetables. This dish freezes very well, so sometimes I will prepare two pans at the same time and freeze one, for those busy times when I want a satisfying supper that can just be popped in the oven without any fuss.

8-oz. pkg. spaghetti, uncooked
3 T. oil
1 lb. lean ground beef
1/2 c. onion, chopped
1/3 c. green pepper, chopped
15-1/2 oz. jar spaghetti sauce

salt and pepper to taste
1/2 c. grated Parmesan cheese
2 eggs, beaten
2 t. butter, diced
1 c. cottage cheese
1 c. shredded mozzarella cheese

Cook spaghetti according to package directions; drain. Meanwhile, in a large skillet over medium heat, combine oil, beef, onion and green pepper. Cook until browned, stirring to break up beef; drain. Stir in spaghetti sauce and heat through. Season with salt and pepper. In a large bowl, combine cooked spaghetti, Parmesan cheese, beaten eggs and butter. Spread spaghetti mixture in a greased 13"x9" baking pan. Spread cottage cheese evenly over top; do not stir. Spread beef mixture over cottage cheese layer; sprinkle with mozzarella cheese. Bake, uncovered, at 350 degrees for 25 to 35 minutes, until bubbly and cheese melts. Serves 8 to 10.

Take it easy when planning large family dinners...stick to tried & true recipes! You'll find your guests are just as happy with simple comfort foods as with the most elegant gourmet meal.

Dill Beef Noodles

Paige Bear
Lyman, SC

This is a favorite of our little girls. It's easy to prepare in a slow cooker. The gravy is delicious over the noodles...we love to sop it up with bread!

1 lb. ground beef
3/4 c. onion
1 clove garlic, minced
2 14-oz. cans beef broth
3 T. Worcestershire sauce
1/4 t. dried dill weed
1/4 t. dried thyme
1/4 t. kosher salt
2 T. cornstarch
2 T. cold water
cooked egg noodles

Brown beef in a skillet over medium heat; add onion and cook until tender. Drain; stir in garlic and cook for 30 seconds. Transfer beef mixture to a 3-quart slow cooker. Add beef broth, Worcestershire sauce and seasonings. Cover and cook on low setting for 6 to 8 hours, or on high setting for 4 hours. In a cup, stir together cornstarch and water. Stir into mixture in slow cooker; cover and turn to high setting for 30 minutes. Serve beef mixture over cooked noodles. Makes 6 servings.

Wide-rimmed soup plates are perfect for serving saucy noodle dishes as well as hearty dinner portions of soup.

Autumn Acorn Squash

Susan Jacobs
Vista, CA

About 15 years ago, while trying to figure out what to do with a couple of acorn squash I'd brought home, I saw a box of stuffing mix in my pantry. I tried this recipe and it was delicious. Since then, I have continued to make this every time I get acorn squash on sale. It's a very quick dish to prepare, about 20 minutes from start to finish. Tasty as a side dish or as a meatless main dish.

2 acorn squash, halved
    and seeded
1 T. olive oil, divided
6 T. butter
1/4 c. onion, diced

1/3 c. celery, diced
pepper to taste
14-oz. can chicken broth
6-oz. pkg. turkey or chicken
    stuffing mix

Brush insides of squash halves with half of olive oil. Place 2 squash halves cut-side up on a microwave-safe plate; microwave for 6 minutes, or until squash is soft and fully cooked. Set aside; repeat with remaining squash halves. Meanwhile, melt butter in a large skillet over medium heat; add onion and celery. Cook until onion is translucent; season with pepper. Add chicken broth; bring to a boil. Add dry stuffing mix and stir until all crumbs are moistened. Remove from heat; season with more pepper, if desired. Scoop stuffing into squash halves. Serve immediately, or if desired, bake in a hot oven until stuffing is crisp on top. Makes 4 servings.

On Turkey Day, set out a bowl of unshelled walnuts or pecans and a nutcracker. Guests will keep busy cracking nuts to snack on while you put the finishing touches on dinner.

Farmhouse Comfort Foods

Company Noodle Casserole

Sharon Welch
LaCygne, KS

This is easy and delicious! Just add a tossed salad and some warm rolls for a wonderful dinner with guests. Great for potlucks too.

4 c. wide egg noodles, uncooked
1 lb. ground beef
1/3 c. onion, chopped
2 8-oz. cans tomato sauce

8-oz. pkg. cream cheese, softened
1 c. cottage cheese
1/4 c. sour cream

Cook noodles according to package directions; drain. Meanwhile, in a skillet over medium heat, brown beef with onion; drain. Stir in tomato sauce; simmer until heated through. Combine remaining ingredients in a bowl; blend well and aside. In a greased 3-quart casserole dish, layer half each of noodles, beef mixture and cottage cheese mixture. Repeat layering. Bake, uncovered, at 350 degrees for 40 minutes, or until bubbly and golden. Makes 6 servings.

Storytelling time! After dinner, invite family members to share their most treasured family stories. Be sure to save these special moments by capturing them on video.

Autumn Recipes from the Farmhouse

Yummy Sloppy Joes

Monica Pedelty Simpson
Burlington, NC

This is a recipe from a child's cookbook that was given to me by my grandparents when I was eight years old. My mom and I added a few ingredients to suit our family's taste. My husband, who does not care for ground beef, loves these sandwiches! It is a quick & easy weekday fix.

1 lb. ground beef
1 c. catsup
3 T. brown sugar, packed
2 T. mustard
2 T. cider vinegar
1/2 t. garlic powder
1/2 t. onion salt
1 t. Worcestershire sauce
6 to 8 hamburger buns, split

Brown beef in a deep skillet over medium heat; drain. Stir in remaining ingredients except buns. Simmer for about 5 to 10 minutes, stirring occasionally, until sauce is slightly thickened. Spoon onto buns and serve. Makes 6 to 8 sandwiches.

Cheddar-Filled Burgers

Liz Sulak
Rosenberg, TX

These tasty cheese-filled hamburgers are great for picnics.

2 lbs. lean ground beef
1/2 c. onion, finely chopped
2 t. Worcestershire sauce
2 t. dry mustard
1 t. salt
1 t. pepper
6 slices Cheddar cheese
6 hamburger buns, split
Garnish: mustard, catsup, pickle relish

In a large bowl, combine all ingredients except cheese, buns and garnish. Mix well; form into 12 very thin patties. Top each of 6 patties with a cheese slice and another patty; gently press edges together. Grill or pan-fry as desired. Serve burgers on buns with favorite toppings. Makes 6 sandwiches.

Party in
the Barn

Spicy Corn Dip

Courtney Stultz
Weir, KS

*I love being able to use fresh garden vegetables in any dish!
This features fresh corn and peppers...it's a great appetizer
any time of year. Serve with tortilla or corn chips.*

3 slices turkey bacon, diced
1/2 c. onion, diced
2 ears sweet corn, cooked and
   sliced from cob, or 15-oz. can
   corn, drained
2 jalapeño peppers, finely diced

1 c. sour cream
1 t. sea salt
1/2 t. pepper
1/2 t. dried sage
1/4 c. shredded Cheddar cheese

In a skillet over medium heat, sauté bacon with onion until bacon is
crisp; drain and set aside. In a bowl, combine corn, jalapeños, sour
cream, seasonings and bacon mixture. Mix until well combined. Spoon
mixture into a lightly greased one-quart casserole baking dish. Sprinkle
with cheese. Bake, uncovered, at 350 degrees for about 10 minutes,
until cheese is melted. Serve warm or chilled. Serves 6 to 8.

Stir up some old-fashioned fun this Halloween. Light the house
with spooky candlelight and serve homemade popcorn balls,
pumpkin cookies and hot cider. Bob for apples and play pin the tail
on the black cat...kids of all ages will love it!

Party in the Barn

Black-Eyed Pea Salsa

Pat Martin
Riverside, CA

I first tasted this colorful salsa at a First Baptist Church choir dinner in 1994. It was amazing! Since then, I have been making this recipe every Christmas as a healthy dip for veggies or chips. It balances out all the other holiday goodies we consume! This salsa can also be served in small dishes as a veggie side dish, or even spooned into pitas like a relish.

16-oz. can black-eyed peas,
   drained
15-oz. can corn, drained
1/2 c. red pepper, diced
1/2 c. red onion, diced
1/4 to 1/2 c. favorite salsa

1/2 t. salt
pepper to taste
3 to 4 T. olive oil
3 to 4 T. vinegar
Optional: tortilla or corn chips

In a large bowl, combine black-eyed peas, corn, red pepper, red onion, salsa, salt and pepper; stir. Add 3 tablespoons each olive oil and vinegar; stir, taste and add remaining oil and/or vinegar, if desired. Cover and refrigerate several hours or overnight. Serve with tortilla or corn chips, or as a side dish. Makes 5 cups.

A hollowed-out pumpkin is a fun way to serve favorite dips.
Set it on a serving tray and surround with a variety of crackers
and veggie dippers.

Autumn Recipes from the Farmhouse

Pumpernickel Loaf Dill Dip

Doreen Knapp
Stanfordville, NY

My mom and auntie just loved pumpernickel bread! Every time one of them had made this, you would see the two of them eating and standing around the table. The recipe brings back so many memories of them both.

2 16-oz. containers sour cream
1/2 c. mayonnaise
1/2 c. dried, minced onions
2 to 3 T. dill seed
1 T. dried parsley
1 large loaf pumpernickel bread

In a large bowl, mix together all ingredients except bread. Cover and chill for 4 to 6 hours or overnight. Meanwhile, cut out center of loaf to form a bowl. Cube the cut-out bread. At serving time, spoon dip into bread bowl; serve with bread cubes for dipping. Serves 6.

Best Bacon-Cheese Ball

Ann Davis
Brookville, IN

This stuff is very addictive! Serve with your favorite crackers.

2 8-oz. pkgs. cream cheese, softened
1/2 c. shredded Cheddar cheese
1-oz. pkg. ranch salad dressing mix
1/4 t. cayenne pepper
1 lb. bacon, crisply cooked, crumbled and divided
Optional 1/4 c. green onions, diced

In a large bowl, mix together cheeses, dressing mix, cayenne pepper, 1/4 cup crumbled bacon and onions, if using. Form into a ball. Wrap in plastic wrap; chill. Just before serving, roll ball in remaining crumbled bacon until well coated. Serves 8 to 12.

Cheese balls can be made several days ahead of time and refrigerated. Roll in nuts or other crisp coating just before serving.

Party in the Barn

Hot Artichoke & Feta Cheese Dip

Delores Lakes
Mansfield, OH

Very simple, easy to assemble and tasty! I like to serve it with shredded wheat crackers, pita chips or Melba toast.

14-oz. can artichoke hearts, drained and finely chopped
6-oz. container crumbled feta cheese
2/3 c. mayonnaise
1/4 c. grated Parmesan cheese
2 T. diced pimentos, drained
2 t. garlic, minced

In a bowl, stir all ingredients until well combined. Transfer mixture to a 9" glass pie plate. Bake, uncovered, at 350 degrees for 25 minutes, or until lightly golden. Let cool for about 5 minutes before serving. Serves 8.

Easy Garden Bruschetta

Christy Smith
Grove City, PA

I make this treat when my roma tomatoes are ripe. You can use storebought tomatoes, but those just out of the garden are extra yummy.

4 to 5 ripe roma tomatoes, diced
1/4 c. onion, diced
4 cloves garlic, thinly sliced
1/2 c. fresh basil, finely chopped, or 1 T. dried basil
5 T. olive oil, divided
1 loaf crusty Italian bread, sliced
salt and pepper to taste

Combine tomatoes, onion, garlic and basil in a bowl. Stir in 3 tablespoons olive oil until vegetables are coated. Cover and refrigerate. Shortly before serving time, brush sliced bread on one side with remaining oil; arrange on a broiler pan. Broil until lightly golden; turn over slices and broil other side. Place bowl of tomato mixture in the center of a large platter. Arrange bread slices around the bowl, so guests can spoon their own topping onto the bread. Serves 8 to 10.

Autumn Recipes
from the Farmhouse

Bacon & Cheesy Zucchini Bites

Laurie Ellithorpe
Weeki Wachee, FL

*This is a perfect snack for the early birds who arrive before dinner!
I find everything fresh from my garden...but luckily all the
veggies are available year 'round at the supermarket too.*

2 c. zucchini, shredded
1 t. salt
1 c. mayonnaise
1/4 c. grated Parmesan cheese
1/4 c. green pepper, finely diced
4 green onions, chopped

1 clove garlic, minced
1 t. Worcestershire sauce
1/4 t. hot pepper sauce
1 loaf party rye bread
2.8-oz. pkg. real bacon bits

In a large bowl, mix all ingredients except bread and bacon bits. Cover
and chill, if not serving right away. To serve, spoon mixture onto bread
slices; sprinkle with bacon bits. Arrange on a baking sheet. Bake at
350 degrees for 10 to 15 minutes, until golden. Serve immediately.
Makes about 3 dozen.

The leaves had a wonderful frolic.
They danced to the wind's loud song.
They whirled, and they floated, and they scampered.
They circled and flew along.

–Anonymous

Party in the Barn

Mom's Candied Chicken Wings

*Joan Baker
Westland, MI*

My mom found this recipe in a magazine and decided to try it, even though she wasn't really a fan of chicken wings. It ended up being one of our favorites. Warning! This can be very messy and sticky to eat, but you won't mind the mess once you have tasted these wings. It also can be served with steamed rice as a meal. Yum!

3 lbs. chicken wings
salt and pepper to taste
1/2 c. regular or light soy sauce
1/2 c. catsup

1/2 c. honey
1/4 c. brown sugar, packed
1 clove garlic, pressed

Pat chicken wings dry with paper towels. Tuck wing tips underneath, or cut wings into 3 pieces, discarding wing tips. Arrange wings in a greased 13"x9" glass baking pan. Season with salt and pepper; set aside. Combine remaining ingredients in a bowl; mix well and spoon over wings. Bake, uncovered, at 350 degrees for 45 minutes, basting with sauce in pan every 15 minutes. Remove from oven; let stand for 10 minutes before serving. Serves 4.

Throw a pumpkin painting party. Provide acrylic paints, brushes and plenty of pumpkins...invite kids to bring their imagination and an old shirt to wear as a smock. Parents are sure to join in too!

Autumn Recipes
from the Farmhouse

Deviled Egg Spread

Nancy Wise
Little Rock, AR

My family loves deviled eggs, but somehow the eggs never seem to peel neatly. So I was happy to discover this recipe. It has all the scrumptious flavor of deviled eggs minus the frustration! Serve with sliced vegetables and triangles of toast.

1 doz. eggs, hard-boiled, peeled
   and divided
3/4 c. reduced-fat mayonnaise
1/2 c. Neufchâtel cheese,
   softened

2 T. white vinegar
1 T. Dijon mustard
3 green onions, sliced
   and divided
Garnish: paprika

Set aside one hard-boiled egg for garnish; cut remaining eggs in half. Remove yolks and place in a food processor. Add 12 egg white halves, mayonnaise, cheese, vinegar and mustard; process until blended. Spoon into a large bowl. Coarsely chop remaining egg whites and add to mixture along with 2/3 of the onions; mix lightly. Finely chop reserved egg; sprinkle over egg mixture in bowl along with remaining onions. Sprinkle with paprika. Serves 8 to 10.

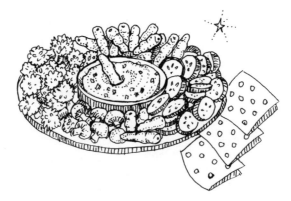

Try something new with your next bowl of veggie dip!
Slices of yellow summer squash, romaine lettuce leaves
and even lightly steamed green beans, snow peas and
asparagus spears are tasty and crunchy.

Party in the Barn

Ham & Cheese Pretzel Bites
Cassie Hooker
La Porte, TX

This is a warm, tasty snack for any kind of party! It makes a great after-school snack too.

2 11-oz. tubes refrigerated bread
   stick dough
2 t. Dijon mustard
1 c. thick-sliced deli baked ham,
   finely chopped

1 c. shredded Cheddar cheese
1 egg, beaten
2 T. butter, melted
coarse or kosher salt to taste

Unroll both tubes of dough. Lay out into 2 long pieces side-by-side on a floured surface. Lightly roll dough into a single 12-inch by 4-inch rectangle. Brush lightly with mustard; sprinkle with ham and cheese. With one long side facing you, gently press ham and cheese into the bottom third of dough. Roll up as tightly as possible, starting with filled end. Cut into 12, one-inch pieces; transfer to a parchment paper-lined baking sheet. Brush lightly with egg. Bake at 375 degrees for about 15 minutes, until puffed and golden. Immediately brush with melted butter; sprinkle with coarse salt. Serve warm. Makes one dozen.

Sparkling Cranberry Punch
Diana Chaney
Olathe, KS

So easy to make...so festive and refreshing!

6-oz. can frozen pink lemonade,
   thawed

8 c. cranberry juice cocktail
1 qt. seltzer water, chilled

Combine lemonade and cranberry juice in a large pitcher; stir and refrigerate. At serving time, add seltzer water and serve. Makes 3 quarts.

Be on the lookout for ice cube trays in whimsical shapes... autumn leaf and pumpkin ice cubes would be such fun floating in punch!

Sweet-and-Sour Meatballs

Sheila Plock
Leland, NC

This makes a scrumptious party appetizer for an open house,
or for watching the big game on TV. It can be kept warm
in a slow cooker set on the low setting.

1 lb. ground beef
1 lb. ground hot pork sausage

1 onion, diced
1 green pepper, diced

In a large bowl, combine all ingredients. Mix well; shape into one-inch meatballs. Add meatballs to a skillet over medium heat. Cook, turning often, until browned and no longer pink in the center. In a colander, rinse meatballs with hot water to remove any excess grease. Add meatballs to Sauce in pan. Reduce heat to low; simmer for 20 minutes. Serves 16 to 20.

Sauce:

1/2 c. brown sugar, packed
1/2 c. catsup

1/4 c. cider vinegar

In a large saucepan over medium heat, combine all ingredients. Cook, stirring often, until bubbly and brown sugar dissolves.

Partying outdoors? Fill a large galvanized tub
with ice, then nestle in bottles of soda.
Everyone can help themselves!

Party in the Barn

Hot Dogs in Mustard Sauce

Karen Thaler
Zephyrhills, FL

The first time I tasted this, back in 1974, it was served as an appetizer in a fondue pot. I still take it to potluck dinners and always bring home an empty pot. My family loves it served as the main dish...serve with potato puffs, topped with some of the sauce.

2 to 3 lbs. favorite hot dogs   3/4 c. mustard
12-oz. jar red currant jelly

Cut hot dogs into bite-size pieces; set aside. In a large saucepan over medium-low heat, melt jelly and mustard; stir until blended. Add hot dogs; mix well. (Sauce won't cover hot dogs, but that's all right.) Simmer over low heat at least one hour, stirring occasionally. If possible, cover and refrigerate overnight; reheat the next day for serving. Freezes well. Serves 8 to 10.

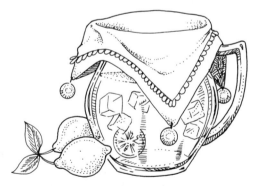

Stir up a frosty pitcher of lemonade. Combine 3 cups water, 1/2 cup sugar and 1/2 cup fresh-squeezed lemon juice. Stir until sugar dissolves and serve over ice...wonderful!

Autumn Recipes from the Farmhouse

All-Time Favorite Hot Cheese Dip

Lisa Hains
Ontario, Canada

Of all my appetizer recipes, this one is #1, and the most loved! Excellent served alongside soup and rolls for a special luncheon.

1 c. mayonnaise
1 c. sour cream
3 c. shredded Cheddar cheese
3/4 c. grated Parmesan cheese
2 T. onion or vegetable soup mix
1/2 t. garlic powder

1/2 t. dried basil
salt and pepper to taste
Garnish: 1/2 c. bacon, crisply
   cooked and crumbled
crackers, bread slices, pretzel
   rods, cut-up vegetables

In a large bowl, stir together mayonnaise, sour cream, cheeses, soup mix and seasonings. Spread in a lightly greased 9" glass pie plate; sprinkle with crumbled bacon. Bake, uncovered, at 350 degrees for 25 to 35 minutes, until bubbly and golden. Serve with dippers as desired. Makes 8 to 10 servings.

For a fancier presentation: Arrange a pie crust in a 9" tart pan with a removable bottom. Spoon filling into crust. Optional add-ins: chopped cooked chicken, finely chopped artichoke hearts, mushrooms and/or peppers. Garnish with crumbled bacon. Bake at 350 degrees for 45 minutes. Cool 10 minutes before cutting into wedges.

Collect autumn leaves to use as coasters for a burst of color on the dinner table. Write guests' names along the edge with a gold or copper paint pen...they'll double as placecards too.

Party in the Barn

Lynda's Texas Salsa

Lynda Kennedy
Pearland, TX

After trying many recipes and tweaking each one, I came up with my own version of salsa. It's yummy! Choose the size of your jalapeño pepper according to how spicy or mild you want the salsa to be. Serve with crisp tortilla chips.

14-1/2 oz. can petite diced
   tomatoes
2 large or 3 small chunks pickled
   banana peppers
1 whole jalapeño pepper, stem
   trimmed
2 T. onion, minced

juice of 1 small lime
1/2 t. garlic, minced
1/4 t. ground cumin
1/8 t. cayenne pepper
1/8 t. dried cilantro, or to taste
salt and pepper to taste

Add all ingredients to a food processor. Process until well blended but not puréed, turning it on and off to desired consistency. Serve immediately, or cover and chill. Makes about 2 cups.

Vintage-style wooden cutting boards in fun shapes like pigs, fish or roosters make whimsical party snack servers.

Autumn Recipes
from the Farmhouse

Wendy Lee's Caramelized Onion Spread

Wendy Lee Paffenroth
Pine Island, NY

*Living in a farming area where lots of onions are grown,
I decided to try something new for our hunting camp picnic.
This delicious spread was gone quickly!*

1/4 to 1/2 c. butter
2 to 3 T. olive oil
4 to 5 onions, chopped
1/4 to 1/2 c. whiskey, sweet
   vermouth or white grape juice
16-oz. container sour cream

3 8-oz. pkgs. cream cheese,
   softened
1/4 c. mayonnaise
hot pepper sauce or prepared
   horseradish to taste
crackers or sliced vegetables

Melt butter with olive oil in a skillet over medium-low heat. Add onions and whiskey, vermouth or juice to skillet. Increase heat to medium-high. Cook, stirring often, until caramelized and deeply golden, but not burnt. Transfer onions to a colander to drain. Pat with paper towels to remove more of the grease; set aside. In a large bowl, combine remaining ingredients except crackers or vegetables. Add onion mixture; beat with an electric mixer on medium speed until smooth. Cover and chill for several hours or overnight. Serve with crackers or sliced vegetables. Serves 10 to 12.

Treat yourself to a jolly Jack-o'-Lantern shake! In a blender, combine 3 scoops vanilla ice cream, 2 tablespoons canned pumpkin, 1/4 cup milk and 1/4 teaspoon pumpkin pie spice. Process until smooth. Pour into 2 tall glasses and share with a friend.

Party in the Barn

Spicy Squash Pickles

Connie Hilty
Pearland, TX

My family & friends all love these crisp, quick pickles! They're perfect for a holiday relish plate, or just tuck 'em into a burger bun.

3/4 lb. yellow squash, sliced
   1/4-inch thick
3/4 lb. zucchini, sliced 1/4-inch
   thick
2 t. kosher salt, divided

1/2 c. sweet onion, thinly sliced
1 c. water
1 c. cider vinegar
1/4 c. pure maple syrup
1/4 to 1/2 t. red pepper flakes

Set a wire rack on a baking sheet. Arrange squash and zucchini slices on rack; sprinkle with one teaspoon salt. Let stand 30 minutes; transfer to a colander and rinse well with cold water. Pat dry with paper towels. Combine zucchini, squash and onion in a glass bowl and set aside. In a small saucepan, combine water, remaining salt, vinegar, maple syrup and pepper flakes. Bring to a boil over medium-high heat; stir well and pour over vegetables. Set a plate over vegetables to weigh them down. Refrigerate at least 2 hours or overnight. Drain, or serve with a slotted spoon. Serves 10 to 12.

For an easy party spread guests will love, serve up a festive charcuterie board. That's fancy talk for a meat & cheese tray! Arrange a selection of smoked or cured deli meats, cheeses, crackers, nuts, fresh or dried fruits...even some gourmet mustard and preserves for dipping. Delicious and such fun!

Autumn Recipes from the Farmhouse

Mom's Cinnamon Apples

Joyce Keeling
Republic, MO

My mom was crazy about cinnamon apples. Every year, as soon as the Golden Delicious apples were available, she'd make her cinnamon apples. I can still remember the smell of them cooking on the stove and waiting for them to cool enough for that first taste! She'd have them on the table for every meal, but loved them most alongside her spaghetti.

1-2/3 c. white vinegar
3-1/4 c. sugar
1 c. red cinnamon candies
3 to 4 drops red food coloring

4 lbs. Golden Delicious apples, peeled
4 1-pint canning jars with lids, sterilized

Combine all ingredients except apples in a large saucepan over medium heat. Bring to a boil; simmer until candies are dissolved. Reduce heat to medium-low. Meanwhile, slice apples crosswise into rings; remove the cores. (Apples can also be cut into chunks.) Add apples to syrup, a few at a time. Cook until barely tender, turning occasionally, about 5 minutes. Divide apples evenly among jars and cover with hot syrup, leaving 1/2-inch headspace. Wipe rims; secure with lids and rings. Process in a boiling water bath for 15 minutes; set jars on a towel to cool. Check for seals. Let stand one week before serving. Makes 4 pints.

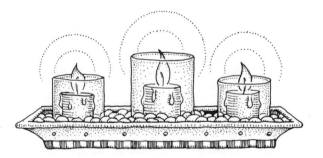

For a quick & easy centerpiece, set lighted votives on a shallow tray filled with acorns, glass pebbles or even candy corn.

Party in the Barn

Jen's Marinated Vegetables

Jen Thomas
Santa Rosa, CA

This takes just minutes to put together. Tuck it in the fridge, ready to serve later! Choose all your favorite veggies...broccoli, carrots, cauliflower, cherry tomatoes, zucchini and tiny Brussels sprouts are all tasty.

4 c. assorted fresh vegetables,
   cubed or sliced
1/4 c. lemon juice
1/4 c. oil

1 T. sugar
1/2 t. dried oregano
1 t. salt
1/8 t. pepper

Combine all vegetables in a shallow bowl; set aside. Combine remaining ingredients in a small jar. Cover and shake well; pour over vegetables. Cover and refrigerate for 6 hours, stirring occasionally. Makes 4 cups.

Marinated Mushrooms

Darcy Hancock
Nunnelly, TN

A friend shared this recipe years ago on a Thanksgiving camping trip. I scaled it down to include just the mushrooms and dressing, but you could add some snipped herbs, if you like.

1 lb. whole mushrooms, halved
   or quartered
0.7-oz. pkg. Italian salad
   dressing mix

1/4 c. white vinegar
3 T. water
1/2 c. oil

Add mushrooms to a large jar with a lid; set aside. Prepare dressing mix with vinegar, water and oil according to package directions. Pour enough dressing over mushrooms to cover. Add lid; stand jar on end or rotate it around so all mushrooms are cover with dressing. This does not require refrigeration, but will keep longer if refrigerated. Makes 4 to 6 servings.

Serve favorite dips with vegetable chips...they can be found
in fall colors like orange, red and gold.

Holiday Cranberry Spread

Jill Ball
Highland, UT

This is an easy, yummy treat. I keep the ingredients on hand during the holidays, then if someone pops in, I have something festive and beautiful to serve. It is also good on leftover turkey sandwiches.

12-oz. pkg. fresh cranberries
1 c. sugar
1 c. apricot preserves
1 c. chopped pecans

8-oz. pkg. cream cheese, softened
assorted crackers

Combine cranberries and sugar in a bowl; toss well. Spread on an ungreased baking sheet and cover with aluminum foil. Bake at 350 degrees for about one hour, until cranberries burst. Remove from oven; transfer cranberry mixture to a bowl. Add preserves and pecans; stir well. Cover and refrigerate until serving time. To serve, unwrap cream cheese and place on a serving plate; spoon cranberry mixture over cream cheese. Serve with crackers. Serves 10 to 12.

Kids will love making some turkey track snacks! Spread softened cheese spread on a cracker and arrange three chow mein noodles on top for the "track." Place on a platter for tasty nibbling.

Party in the Barn

Acorn Squash Dip

Linda Duffy
Mashpee, MA

I served this at a holiday gathering...they couldn't keep away from the dip! Serve with pita chips.

2 acorn squash, halved and
   seeds removed
1/2 c. milk
1 clove garlic, minced

1 t. brown mustard
1/4 c. shredded Cheddar cheese
1/2 c. crumbled blue cheese
salt and pepper to taste

Arrange squash halves on an ungreased baking sheet, cut-side up. Bake at 400 degrees for about one hour, until fork-tender. Cool slightly; scoop out pulp and mash. In a saucepan over low heat, combine milk, garlic and mustard. Add squash pulp and cheeses; cook and stir until cheeses melt. Season with salt and pepper; serve warm. Serves 6.

Apple Honey Dip

Kathy Fehr
Fairbury, IL

This is a favorite for our fall get-togethers...it's so yummy!

3/4 c. creamy peanut butter
1/4 c. butter, softened
1/4 c. honey

1 t. vanilla extract
sliced apples

Combine peanut butter, butter, honey and vanilla in a bowl. Beat with an electric mixer on medium speed until blended. Cover and refrigerate. Before serving, let stand at room temperature to soften. Serve with sliced apples. Will keep a long time refrigerated. Makes about 1-1/4 cups.

Pick up a dozen pint-size canning jars...they're perfect for serving cold beverages at farmhouse-style gatherings.

Autumn Recipes from the Farmhouse

Confetti Spread

Barb Bargdill
Gooseberry Patch

This creamy, veggie-packed spread is delicious on snack crackers.

8-oz. pkg. cream cheese,
   softened
8-oz. pkg. finely shredded sharp
   Cheddar cheese
1/2 c. mayonnaise
2 t. dried parsley

3/4 c. green olives with
   pimentos, chopped
1/2 c. celery, chopped
1/3 c. onion, chopped
1/4 c. green pepper, chopped

In a large bowl, beat cheeses and mayonnaise with an electric mixer on medium speed until smooth. Fold in remaining ingredients, mixing just enough to evenly combine. Cover and chill for at least one hour. Makes 15 servings.

Sage Sausage Balls

Sheila Gwaltney
Johnson City, TN

I have served these at bridal and baby shower brunches and they're always a hit. Perfect for any kind of party, really! They're also good made with a pound each of hot sausage and country sausage.

2 lbs. ground pork sage sausage
1 c. apple, cored and chopped
1 c. stuffing mix

1/2 c. milk
1/2 c. onion, chopped
2 eggs, beaten

In a large bowl, mix all ingredients together. Grease 12 muffin cups or 36 mini muffin cups. Lightly press mixture into cups. Bake at 350 degrees, 45 minutes for large muffin cups or 20 minutes for mini muffin cups. Recipe may be doubled or tripled and frozen, then thawed and reheated. Makes one dozen large balls or 3 dozen small balls.

Crackers will stay crisper if they're served in a basket separate from dips or spreads, not on the same platter.

Cool Cucumber Dip

Marlene Burns
Swisher, IA

I found this recipe in a recipe folder I inherited from my sister Marlys. It's a quick, fun dip to serve with fresh vegetables. She has passed away, but will be remembered for her great cooking.

3/4 c. cucumber, peeled, seeded
   and cubed
1/2 c. onion, chopped
8-oz. pkg. cream cheese, cubed

1/2 c. mayonnaise
2 to 3 T. Western salad dressing
1/2 to 1 t. celery seed
1/2 t. garlic salt or powder

Combine all ingredients in a blender or food processor. Process until smooth. Transfer to a serving bowl; cover and chill until serving time. Makes about 2 cups.

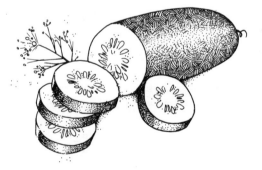

Spice up your favorite ranch salad dressing. To one cup of ranch salad dressing, whisk in 1/2 teaspoon ground cumin and 1/4 teaspoon chili powder. Let stand a few minutes for flavors to blend. Divine for dipping...super for salads!

Autumn Recipes from the Farmhouse

Tasty Bread Tarts

Janis Parr
Ontario, Canada

These appetizers are sure to be a hit with everyone! They are scrumptious and fun to make too.

18 slices white bread, crusts
    trimmed and reserved
1/2 c. butter, softened
1-1/2 lbs. lean ground beef
10-3/4 oz. can cream of
    mushroom soup
2 eggs, well beaten

3/4 c. shredded Cheddar cheese
1-1/2 T. dried, minced onions
1-1/4 t. Worcestershire sauce
1/2 t. dried basil
1/2 t. salt
1/4 t. pepper

Spread trimmed bread slices with butter. Press one piece of buttered bread into each of 18 muffin cups, butter-side down. In a food processor, process reserved crusts into crumbs. In a large bowl, combine crumbs, uncooked beef and remaining ingredients. Mix well; fill muffin cups with beef mixture. Bake at 350 degrees for 30 minutes, or until filling is cooked through. Makes 1-1/2 dozen.

For a sweet & salty party snack that's ready in minutes, serve a tub of caramel apple dip with crunchy apple slices and mini pretzel twists. Yummy!

Party in the Barn

Parmesan Spinach Balls

Paula Marchesi
Auburn, PA

Football is a must with me in my house. I enjoy it tremendously and I prepare for it days in advance. I love making all sorts of delicious goodies for all of us to enjoy. It saves me from actually fixing a sit-down meal! Some weekends, there's so much to snack on that we overindulge! This is one of our favorites.

2 10-oz. pkgs. frozen chopped spinach	1/2 c. grated Parmesan cheese
3 c. herb-seasoned stuffing mix	1-1/2 t. garlic salt
1 c. onion, chopped	1 t. chipotle chili pepper
6 eggs, well beaten	1 t. pepper
	1/2 t. Dijon mustard

Cook spinach according to package directions; drain well and transfer to a large bowl. Add remaining ingredients; mix well. Shape into tiny balls, about one inch. Place balls on lightly greased baking sheets. Bake at 350 degrees for 15 to 20 minutes, until cooked through. Arrange in a serving dish, with toothpicks on the side. Makes about 10 dozen tiny balls.

Host a tailgating cook-off! Invite all the neighbors to bring their own game-day specialty like chili, chicken wings or barbecued ribs. You provide the beverages, baskets of warm cornbread and plenty of napkins, plus tables for picnicking. Have a prize for the winner!

Autumn Recipes from the Farmhouse

Spicy Pickled Peaches

Sue Klapper
Muskego, WI

This delicious relish recipe comes from a friend's grandmother.

29-oz. can peach halves in
  syrup, drained and one cup
  syrup reserved
0.62-oz. jar whole cloves

1/2 c. sugar
1/2 c. white wine vinegar
4-inch cinnamon stick

Cut each peach half in half again. Stud each piece with 2 cloves. Place peaches in a heatproof bowl; set aside. In a saucepan over medium heat, stir together reserved peach syrup, sugar and vinegar; add cinnamon stick. Bring to a boil; reduce heat to medium-low. Simmer, uncovered, until sugar dissolves. Pour hot syrup over peaches. Cover and refrigerate overnight, or up to several weeks. Makes about one quart.

Orange Crush Punch

Gladys Kielar
Whitehouse, OH

The Ursuline sisters of Toledo, Ohio always served this punch at school functions. More than 40 years later, I'm still making it.

2 qts. orange soda
12-oz. can frozen orange juice
  concentrate, thawed

2 qts. lemon-lime soda, chilled
1 qt. cream soda, chilled

Pour orange soda into a ring mold; freeze until solid. At serving time, combine remaining ingredients in a punch bowl; mix gently. Add frozen ice ring to punch bowl. Serves 20.

For stand-up parties, make it easy on guests by serving foods that can be eaten in just one or 2 bites.

Party in the Barn

Sweet Dill Pickles

Crystal Shook
Catawba, NC

These pickles are great on hamburgers, in chicken salad, egg salad, potato salad or for snacking! They are great as a gift, with a pretty ribbon tied around the jar...you may want to make extra.

1/2 gal. jar whole dill pickles, drained
4 cloves garlic, sliced
4 c. sugar
2 c. cider vinegar

12 whole cloves
3-inch cinnamon stick
3 1-pint canning jars with lids, sterilized

Slice pickles into a large heatproof bowl; add garlic and set aside. In a saucepan, combine sugar, vinegar, cloves and cinnamon stick. Bring to a boil over high heat; simmer for 5 minutes, stirring until sugar dissolves. Pour hot liquid over pickles in bowl. Let cool; discard cloves and cinnamon stick. Divide pickles evenly among jars, leaving 1/2-inch headspace. Pour in enough of the liquid to cover pickles. Add lids. Store in the refrigerator; shake everyday for 10 days before serving. Makes 3 pints.

Have an appetizer swap with friends! Each makes a big batch of their favorite dip, spread or finger food, then get together to sample and divide 'em up. You'll all have a super variety of goodies for the holiday party season.

Autumn Recipes from the Farmhouse

Pumpkin Spice Popcorn

Kimberly Beebe
Independence, IA

A tasty fall snack for popcorn and pumpkin spice fans!

2 T. brown sugar, packed
2 T. pure maple syrup
1-1/2 t. pumpkin pie spice

1 T. butter
5 c. popped popcorn
Optional: 1/2 c. chopped pecans

In a large saucepan, combine brown sugar, maple syrup and spice over medium heat. Cook and stir for 3 minutes, or until bubbly and brown sugar is dissolved. Stir in butter until melted. Add popcorn and pecans, if using; stir until well coated. Allow mixture to cool before serving. Store in an airtight container. Makes 5 cups.

Buttery Walnuts

Leona Krivda
Belle Vernon, PA

Something tasty to do with those freshly gathered walnuts you bought at the fall festival! Always nice to have on hand for snacks.

1 lb. walnut halves
1 T. seasoned salt

1/4 c. butter, sliced

Place walnut halves in a lightly buttered 1-1/2 quart casserole dish. Sprinkle with seasoned salt; dot with butter. Microwave on high setting for 4 to 5 minutes. Stir well to coat evenly; spread on wax paper to cool. Break up any chunks; store in an airtight container. Makes one pound.

Set out serve-yourself portions of snack mixes in mini canning jars or short tumblers.

Party in the Barn

Caramel-ly Apple Cider

Amy Jones
Morgantown, WV

This is the first thing my daughters ask for when the scent of fall appears in the air. It's topped with caramel whipped cream... can't get much better!

3/4 c. whipping cream, divided
1/4 c. plus 1 T. brown sugar,
   packed and divided

3 c. apple cider
1/2 c. water
Optional: cinnamon

In a large saucepan, combine 1/4 cup cream and 1/4 cup brown sugar. Bring to a boil; cook and stir until brown sugar melts and resembles caramel. Reduce heat slightly. Stir in cider and water; bring to a simmer. Do not boil. For whipped cream, place remaining cream in a deep bowl. With an electric mixer on medium-high speed, gradually beat in remaining brown sugar; beat until soft peaks form. Pour cider into mugs. Dollop with whipped cream; sprinkle with cinnamon, if desired. Makes 3 to 4 servings.

Pick up some new paper paint pails from the hardware store to decorate with cut-outs and paint. Fill with snack mix or popcorn and wrap up in clear cellophane...yum!

Autumn Recipes
from the Farmhouse

Creamy Chicken Spread

Jill Valentine
Jackson, TN

This yummy spread can be whipped up in a jiffy! I like to give the bowl a sprinkle of paprika just before serving.

8-oz. pkg. cream cheese,
  softened
1/2 c. sour cream
1 t. dried, minced onions
1/2 t. onion salt

1/2 t. Worcestershire sauce
1/4 t. cayenne pepper
2 10-oz. cans chicken, drained
  and flaked
round buttery crackers

In a large bowl, combine all ingredients except chicken and crackers; blend well. Add chicken and stir well, breaking up any large pieces. Cover and refrigerate at least one hour before serving. Serve with crackers. Makes 8 to 10 servings.

Pick up some plastic icing cones when you shop for baking supplies.
Filled with party mix, tied with curling ribbon and placed in
a wire cupcake stand, they make fun gifts to keep on hand
for drop-in guests.

Party in the Barn

Mozzarella-Stuffed Meatballs
Janae Mallonee
Marlborough, MA

Delicious meatballs with a surprise inside! Serve with marinara sauce for dipping, or jazz up your regular spaghetti & meatballs.

1-1/2 lbs. ground beef
1.35-oz. pkg. onion soup mix
1 egg, beaten
2 T. Worcestershire sauce

1 T. garlic, minced
salt and pepper to taste
8-oz. pkg. mozzarella cheese,
   cut into 24 cubes

In a large bowl, mix all ingredients except cheese. Shape into 24 balls, forming each ball around a cheese cube. Place meatballs on a greased rimmed baking sheet. Bake at 350 degrees for 20 minutes, or until browned. Makes 2 dozen.

Stuffed Jalapeño Peppers
Donna Riggins
Boaz, AL

These are amazing! Great for any occasion. I fix these during football season.

1 lb. ground pork sausage
8-oz. pkg. cream cheese,
   softened
8 to 10 jalapeño peppers, halved
   and seeded

1/2 to 3/4 c. shredded Cheddar
   cheese

Brown sausage in a skillet over medium heat; drain. Add cream cheese and mix well. Spoon mixture into pepper halves. Arrange on a greased baking sheet. Bake at 350 degrees for 10 to 12 minutes, until bubbly and tender. Top with Cheddar cheese; bake another 3 to 5 minutes, until cheese has melted. Serves 16 to 20.

Turn your favorite cheese ball into a pumpkin with a celery stalk and leaves...simple!

Qutumn Recipes from the Farmhouse

Karen's Fall Trail Mix

Karen Gregg
Ferguson, KY

I have always enjoyed fall treats and a friend of mine had made some Christmas trail mix, which gave me the idea for this tasty fall mix. I just tossed together some of my favorite treats...yum yum! Since you just dump & mix, use the package sizes you like. It makes a great treat for fall get-togethers and Halloween parties.

1 jar dry-roasted peanuts
1 pkg. sweetened dried
   cranberries
1/2 c. dark or golden raisins
1/2 pkg. candy corn
1/2 pkg. candy pumpkins

1/2 pkg. candy-coated chocolates
   in fall colors
1/2 pkg. butterscotch chips
1/2 pkg. mini pretzel twists
   or sticks

Mix together all ingredients in a large bowl. Store in an airtight container. Makes as many servings as you like.

Hot Mulled Cranberry Cider

Wendy Jo Minotte
Duluth, MN

This is a very simple recipe, yet oh-so good! Simple to make in a slow cooker...easy to carry with you in a thermos for fall thrifting or chilly football games. It's the perfect drink for cool autumn days.

8 c. cranberry-apple juice
1 c. brown sugar, packed
2 4-inch cinnamon sticks

1 t. whole allspice
1 t. whole cloves

Combine all ingredients in a 3-quart slow cooker. Stir until brown sugar dissolves. Cover and cook on low setting for 3 to 4 hours, until hot. Remove spices before serving. Makes 8 servings.

Delicious Down-Home Desserts

Harvest Pear Crumb Pie

Sharon Demers
Bruce Crossing, MI

This recipe is just wonderful for a brisk fall evening, served with French vanilla ice cream on the side and a piping-hot cup of coffee.

1/2 c. brown sugar, packed	1/8 t. salt
2 T. cornstarch	1 T. lemon juice
1/2 t. cinnamon	6 c. Bosc or Anjou pears, peeled,
1/4 t. ground ginger	cored and thinly sliced
1/8 t. nutmeg	9-inch pie crust, unbaked

In a large bowl, mix together brown sugar, cornstarch, spices and salt. Sprinkle lemon juice over pear slices; add to brown sugar mixture and toss to mix well. Spoon pears into pie crust. Bake at 400 degrees for 25 minutes. Remove from oven; sprinkle with Crumb Topping and bake 40 minutes longer. During the last 15 minutes of baking, cover edges of pie crust with aluminum foil to prevent getting too dark. Makes 8 servings.

Crumb Topping:

2/3 c. all-purpose flour	1/2 c. cold butter
1/3 c. brown sugar, packed	

Mix together flour and brown sugar. With a pastry blender, cut in butter until mixture is crumbly.

Core apples and pears in a jiffy! Simply cut the fruit in half
and use a melon baller to scoop out the center.

Delicious
Down-Home Desserts

Candy Apple Pie

Daisy Sedalnick
Westminster, CO

This recipe was given to me years ago by a good friend. It was her grandmother's recipe. It is really delicious!

3 to 4 Winesap or Granny Smith apples, peeled, cored and thinly sliced
1/2 c. sugar
1/2 c. brown sugar, packed

3/4 c. all-purpose flour
1/2 c. butter, melted
1 egg, beaten
1/2 c. very hot water

Arrange apple slices in a greased or buttered 8"x8" baking pan, Sprinkle sugar over apples; set aside. In a bowl, combine brown sugar, flour, melted butter and egg; mix well and spread over apples. Drizzle hot water over top. Bake at 325 degrees for one hour, or until crusty and golden on top. Makes 6 servings.

Autumn is time for apple fun. Pick your own apples in an orchard, watch cider being pressed at a cider mill or go to a small-town apple butter stirring. Don't forget to taste!

Chocolate Syrup Brownies

Julie Hendrickson
East Grand Forks, MN

*These are by far the best brownies I've tasted! I take them
to functions and get lots of compliments.*

1/2 c. margarine, softened	4 eggs, beaten
1 c. sugar	16-oz. can chocolate syrup
1 c. all-purpose flour	Optional: 1/2 c. chopped nuts

In a large bowl, mix all ingredients together; batter may be slightly
lumpy. Pour batter into a greased 13"x9" baking pan. Bake at
350 degrees for 20 to 25 minutes. Cool; spread with Frosting and
cut into squares. Makes 2 to 3 dozen.

Frosting:

1 c. sugar	1/3 c. milk
1/4 c. margarine	1 c. semi-sweet chocolate chips
2 t. vanilla extract	

In a saucepan over medium heat, combine all ingredients except
chocolate chips. Bring to a boil; continue boiling while counting to
20 rather slowly. Remove from heat; add chocolate chips. Beat to a
spreadable consistency.

Taking brownies or bar cookies to a get-together? For the most
appealing presentation, cut them at home and arrange on a platter.

Delicious Down-Home Desserts

Cranberry-Coconut Bars

*Gladys Kielar
Whitehouse, OH*

*Our neighbor shared a tray of these yummy, colorful bars with me,
and included the recipe. Now I make them for gifts too. Have this
recipe copied for your guests...they will want a copy.*

1-1/2 c. graham cracker crumbs
1/2 c. butter, melted
1-1/2 c. white chocolate chips
1-1/2 c. sweetened dried
   cranberries

14-oz. can sweetened
   condensed milk
1 c. flaked coconut
1 c. pecan halves

In a bowl, combine graham cracker crumbs and butter. Press into the
bottom of a greased 13"x9" baking pan; set aside. In another bowl,
combine remaining ingredients. Mix well and spread gently over crust.
Bake at 350 degrees for 25 minutes, or until edges are golden. Cool in
pan on a wire rack; cut into bars. Makes 2 dozen.

Invite friends over for "just desserts"...perfect for meeting
fellow school parents or getting together with neighbors after
the trick-or-treaters have made the rounds. Offer 2 or 3 simple
desserts like cobbler, bar cookies and fruit pie, ice cream for
topping and a steamy pot of coffee...they'll love it!

Autumn Recipes from the Farmhouse

Chewy Energy Bars

Cindy LeFebvre
Ontario, Canada

In an effort to eat a little healthier, I created this homemade granola bar, full of wholesome ingredients. My kids absolutely love it!

1/3 c. natural creamy
  peanut butter
1/3 c. honey
2 T. dark brown sugar, packed
2 c. gluten-free quick-cooking
  oats, uncooked

2 T. ground flax seed
1/4 c. salted roasted cashews,
  chopped
1/4 c. chopped walnuts
1/4 c. raisins
1/3 c. semi-sweet chocolate chips

Add peanut butter to a large bowl; set aside. In a small saucepan over low heat, bring honey and brown sugar to a boil. Boil until brown sugar is dissolved, about 30 seconds to one minute. Spoon hot mixture over peanut butter; whisk until smooth. Add oats, flax seed, nuts and raisins; mix well to combine. Cool slightly; add chocolate chips. Spoon into a parchment paper-lined 8"x8" baking pan; press down evenly. Place in the freezer for 15 minutes to set; cut into bars. Makes one dozen.

Make spice-scented pine cones to heap in a bowl...so sweet smelling. Carefully dip pine cones into melted beeswax (old candle ends will work just fine!) and while still warm, roll them in cinnamon, cloves and nutmeg.

Marjorie's Sour Cream Cookies

Amanda Bitting
Papillion, NE

My grandma used to make these big, delicious cookies. The incredible smell filled the whole house. We would always fight over the last bite!

1 t. baking soda	3 eggs, beaten
1 c. sour cream	3-1/2 c. all-purpose flour
1 c. shortening	2 t. nutmeg
2 c. sugar	1 t. salt

In a large bowl, stir baking soda into sour cream until dissolved. Add remaining ingredients; mix well. Drop dough by large spoonfuls onto greased baking sheets. Bake at 375 degrees for about 9 to 11 minutes, until edges are very lightly golden. Makes 3 dozen.

A plate of cookies is a sweet way to say "Thanks!" to a teacher or youth leader...it shows how much you appreciate their talents and time. Wrap 'em up on a vintage flowered china plate, picked up for a song at a yard sale. No need to return the plate!

Autumn Recipes
from the Farmhouse

Boiled Cider Apple Pie

Melanie Lowe
Dover, DE

This old-fashioned pie is a delight! I like to serve it warm,
topped with cinnamon ice cream.

2 c. apple cider
2/3 c. sugar
2 T. cornstarch
2 T. cold water
1 t. cinnamon

6 c. Granny Smith and/or
    Jonathan apples, peeled,
    cored and sliced
2 9-inch pie crusts, unbaked
2 T. butter, sliced

Combine cider and sugar in a large saucepan over high heat; bring to a boil. Boil until cider cooks down to one cup, stirring until sugar dissolves. Mix cornstarch, water and cinnamon in a cup; add to cider mixture. Cook and stir until thickened; remove from heat. Add apples to pan; stir gently and set aside. Arrange one crust in a 9" pie plate. Spoon apple mixture into crust; dot with butter. Add remaining crust; pinch or flute edge to seal. Make several slits with a knife tip to vent. Bake at 375 degrees for 45 to 55 minutes, until bubbly and crust is golden. Cut into wedges. Serves 8.

Most fruit desserts freeze well up to 4 months in advance. Cool completely after baking, then wrap well in plastic wrap and 2 layers of aluminum foil before freezing. To serve, thaw overnight in the fridge, bring to room temperature and rewarm in the oven.

Delicious Down-Home Desserts

Red Raspberry Pie
Karen Wilson
Defiance, OH

Now that red raspberries are available year 'round, I can make this pie all the time. Friends often request it for their birthdays instead of cake...that's how good it is!

9-inch frozen pie crust, unbaked
1 c. sugar
1/4 c. cornstarch
1 T. light corn syrup
3 T. raspberry gelatin mix

1-1/2 c. water
3 6-oz. pkgs. fresh red raspberries
8-oz. container frozen whipped topping, thawed

Bake pie crust according to package directions; set aside to cool. Meanwhile, in a saucepan, combine sugar, cornstarch, corn syrup, gelatin mix and water. Cook over medium heat, stirring constantly, until thickened. Cool; gently fold in raspberries. Spoon into baked crust. Top with whipped topping. Cut into wedges; keep refrigerated. Serves 6 to 8.

Quick Blueberry Crisp
Sharon Crider
Junction City, KS

Yum! Any farm wife would be proud of this dessert.

21-oz. can blueberry pie filling
1/2 c. rolled oats, uncooked
1/2 c. all-purpose flour

1/4 c. brown sugar, packed
Optional: 2 T. chopped walnuts
6 T. margarine

Spoon pie filling into a lightly buttered one-quart casserole dish; set aside. In a bowl, combine oats, flour, brown sugar and walnuts, if using. With a pastry blender or 2 knives, cut in margarine until mixture resembles coarse crumbs. Sprinkle over pie filling. Bake, uncovered, at 375 degrees for 45 minutes, or until bubbly and lightly golden. Makes 4 to 6 servings.

Add some pizzazz to plain sugar cookies. Simply stir some sunflower kernels or dried fruit bits into the dough before baking...yummy!

Autumn Recipes from the Farmhouse

Toffee Cashew Treasures

Mel Chencharick
Julian, PA

This is a crisp cookie that's sure to make everyone smile. Toffee and cashews make a scrumptious combination. Great with your morning cup of coffee!

1 c. butter, softened
1 c. sugar
1 c. brown sugar, packed
2 eggs
1 t. vanilla extract
2 c. all-purpose flour
2 c. old-fashioned oats, uncooked

1/2 t. baking powder
1 t. baking soda
1/2 t. salt
1 c. flaked coconut
1 c. milk chocolate-coated English toffee bits or almond brickle chips
1 c. chopped cashews, toasted

In a large bowl, blend butter and sugars until light and fluffy. Add eggs, one at a time, beating well after each. Beat in vanilla; set aside. In a separate bowl, combine flour, oats, baking powder, baking soda and salt. Gradually add flour mixture to butter mixture; mix well. Stir in remaining ingredients. Drop dough by rounded tablespoons onto ungreased baking sheets, 3 inches apart. Bake at 350 degrees for 12 to 14 minutes, until lightly golden. Cool on baking sheets for 2 minutes; remove cookies to a wire rack. Makes 5 dozen.

Whenever you shop for cookie cutters, candy sprinkles and other baking supplies, toss a few extras in the shopping cart. Soon you'll be able to fill a gift basket for a friend who loves to bake...she'll really appreciate your thoughtfulness!

Delicious Down-Home Desserts

Apple Snickerdoodles

Courtney Stultz
Weir, KS

Snickerdoodles were my grandpa's favorite cookie...one of mine too. A cinnamon-flavored slightly crisp and chewy cookie. Yum! How to make them even better for fall? Add some apple, of course.

1 c. butter, softened
1-1/2 c. sugar, divided
1 c. brown sugar, packed
2 eggs, beaten
1 t. vanilla extract
3 c. all-purpose flour

1/2 t. baking soda
1/2 t. cream of tartar
1/4 t. salt
4 t. cinnamon, divided
1/4 c. apple, peeled, cored and
   finely grated

In a large bowl, combine butter, 1-1/4 cups sugar and brown sugar; mix until creamy. Add eggs and vanilla; stir until smooth. Add flour, baking soda, cream of tartar, salt and 2 teaspoons cinnamon; mix until combined. Fold in grated apple. Cover and refrigerate dough for at least 30 minutes. In a small bowl, combine remaining sugar and cinnamon. Scoop dough into one-inch balls; coat in sugar mixture. Arrange on parchment paper-lined baking sheets. Bake at 350 degrees for about 8 to 10 minutes, until lightly golden. Cool completely on wire racks. Makes 2 dozen.

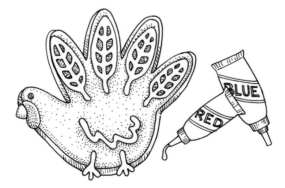

Handprint turkeys...how sweet! Kids place their hands on rolled-out sugar cookie dough, then a grown-up cuts around carefully with a table knife. After the cookies are baked and cooled, kids can decorate their turkeys with tubes of frosting.

Pumpkin Swirl Bread

Jenny Shrider
Daphne, AL

This is a delicious bread that we make every Thanksgiving.
It's very easy to make and your kids will love helping!

1-3/4 c. all-purpose flour
1-1/2 c. sugar
1 t. baking soda
1 t. cinnamon
1/4 t. nutmeg

1/2 t. salt
1 c. canned pumpkin
1/2 c. margarine, melted
1 egg, beaten
1/3 c. water

In a large bowl, combine flour, sugar, baking soda, spices and salt; mix well. Add remaining ingredients; stir until moistened. Reserve 1-3/4 cups batter. Pour remaining batter into a well-greased 9"x5" loaf pan. Top with Filling; add reserved batter. Cut through batter several times with a knife for a swirl effect. Bake at 350 degrees for one hour and 20 minutes, or until bread tests done with a toothpick. Cool 10 minutes; remove from pan. Makes one loaf.

Filling:

8-oz. pkg. cream cheese,
   softened

1/4 c. sugar
1 egg, beaten

Blend cream cheese and sugar. Add egg and mix well.

Plan a fall family outing to a farm. Many are open to the public for good old-fashioned fun like corn mazes, hayrides and pumpkin picking. You'll enjoy it as much as the kids!

Delicious Down-Home Desserts

Triple Layer Chocolate Bars

Jennie Gist
Gooseberry Patch

A deluxe version of everyone's favorite, Hello Dollies!

1-1/2 c. graham cracker crumbs
1/2 c. baking cocoa, divided
1/4 c. sugar
1/3 c. butter, melted
14-oz. can sweetened
   condensed milk
1/4 c. all-purpose flour

1/2 t. baking powder
1 egg, beaten
1 t. vanilla extract
3/4 c. chopped walnuts
12-oz. pkg. semi-sweet chocolate
   chips

In a bowl, mix graham cracker crumbs, 1/4 cup cocoa, sugar and melted butter. Press firmly into the bottom of an ungreased 13"x9" baking pan; set aside. In a large bowl, combine condensed milk, flour, baking powder, remaining cocoa, egg and vanilla. Beat with an electric mixer on medium speed until well blended; fold in walnuts. Spread evenly over crumb crust; sprinkle evenly with chocolate chips. Bake at 350 degrees for 20 to 25 minutes, until set. Cool completely; cut into bars. Store at room temperature, tightly covered. Makes 2 to 3 dozen.

Share your favorite tried & true recipes with a new bride. Jot down recipes on cards, along with your special touches or hints for success. Slip the cards into the pages of a mini photo album and tie with a homespun ribbon. She'll think of you whenever she uses it!

Autumn Recipes from the Farmhouse

Pumpkin Crunch Cream Pie

*Marian Forck
Chamois, MO*

This is a great recipe for Thanksgiving or Christmas...it's sure to be a hit. Use peanut butter chips instead of chocolate chips, if you like.

3/4 c. cold milk
3.4-oz. pkg. instant French
 vanilla pudding mix
8-oz. container frozen whipped
 topping, thawed and divided
1/2 c. canned pumpkin

1/2 c. slivered almonds
1/2 c. semi-sweet chocolate chips
1/4 t. pumpkin pie spice
9-inch graham cracker crust
Optional: additional chocolate
 chips

In a large bowl, combine milk and dry pudding mix. Whisk for 2 minutes, or until thickened. Refrigerate for 5 minutes. Stir in 2 cups whipped topping, pumpkin, almonds, chocolate chips and spice. Spoon into crust; cover and refrigerate at least 4 hours. Garnish with remaining topping and chocolate chips, if desired. Serves 8.

Cadillac Cranberry Pie

*Gladys Kielar
Whitehouse, OH*

Delicious all year long! I freeze bags of cranberries when they are in season and they last all year. Great for Fourth of July or any day.

2 c. fresh or frozen cranberries
1/2 c. chopped walnuts
1-1/2 c. sugar, divided
2 eggs

1 c. all-purpose flour
1/2 c. shortening, melted
1/2 c. butter, melted

Spread cranberries in a lightly greased 10" deep-dish pie plate. Sprinkle with nuts and 1/2 cup sugar; set aside. Beat eggs in a bowl; gradually add remaining sugar and beat thoroughly. Add flour, shortening and butter to sugar mixture; mix well. Pour over cranberries. Bake at 325 degrees for one hour, or until crust is golden. Cut into wedges. Makes 8 servings.

Who can dream of a Thanksgiving dinner without a pie!

-Fannie Farmer

196

Delicious Down-Home Desserts

Delicious Baked Apples

Cassie Hooker
La Porte, TX

I serve these scrumptious baked apples every autumn!
Serve topped with ice cream, if desired.

4 baking apples
1/4 c. brown sugar, packed
2 T. butter, room temperature

1/2 t. cinnamon
1/4 c. chopped walnuts or pecans
1/2 c. water

Using a paring knife, remove the stem and core from each apple, making a deep hole where the filling will go. Do not cut through the bottom. Combine brown sugar, butter and cinnamon in a small bowl. Mix well to combine; stir in nuts. Spoon mixture evenly into each apple. Place apples in an ungreased 8"x8" baking pan; pour water around apples. Bake at 350 degrees for 40 to 45 minutes, until apples are fork-tender. Remove from oven; cool before serving. Makes 4 servings.

Warm caramel topping makes a delightful drizzle over
baked apple pies and cobblers. Just heat it in the microwave
for a few seconds, and it's ready to spoon over desserts.

Autumn Recipes from the Farmhouse

Harvest Day Pie

Linda Shively
Hopkinsville, KY

Several years ago, our family put together a family cookbook. We managed to include every aunt and every first cousin...we had so much fun! It was made extra special because we found a few recipes from my grandmother, Edith Tinius, who passed away more than 60 years ago! This recipe combines two of my favorites...pumpkin and mincemeat. Guess I am just like Grandma!

2-1/2 c. prepared mincemeat
9-inch pie crust, unbaked
1 c. canned pumpkin
1/2 c. brown sugar, packed

1/2 t. cinnamon
1/2 t. nutmeg
1/2 t. salt
2/3 c. milk

Spoon mincemeat into crust; smooth surface with spoon and set aside. Combine pumpkin, sugar, and spices in a bowl; beat well. Add milk and beat again. Spoon pumpkin mixture over mincemeat; smooth surface with spoon. Bake at 450 degrees for 10 minutes. Decrease temperature to 350 degrees; continue baking for 25 minutes. Cool; cut into wedges. Makes 8 servings.

Field pumpkins raised for perfect Jack-o'-Lanterns tend to be too large and stringy for baking. Look for sugar pumpkins instead... a medium-size sugar pumpkin will yield about 1-1/2 cups of cooked, mashed pumpkin. This purée can be used in all your recipes calling for canned pumpkin.

Delicious Down-Home Desserts

Dad's Popcorn Balls

Jean Johns Schmehl
Saint Marys, OH

My dad, John Robert Johns, always made these popcorn balls.
He passed away in 1992 and now my husband and I make them
every year. Such a wonderful treat!

1 c. popcorn, unpopped
Optional: salt to taste
1/2 c. butter

40 regular marshmallows
Optional: few drops desired food
    coloring

Pop corn; place in a heatproof large bowl and remove any unpopped kernels. Season lightly with salt, if desired; set aside. Melt butter in a heavy saucepan over medium heat. Add marshmallows; stir constantly until melted. Add a few drops food coloring, if desired. Stir until well mixed. Pour mixture over popped corn; mix well. With buttered hands, form into balls. Makes about 8 popcorn balls.

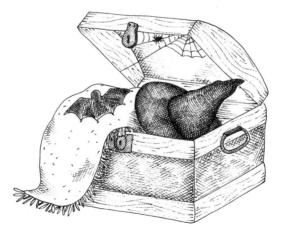

You're never too old to make some Halloween memories!
Invite friends to visit, dress up in thrift-shop costumes and
take pictures, make popcorn balls together and watch all
the old, classic monster movies!

Autumn Recipes from the Farmhouse

Soft Peanut Brittle

Charlene Letterly
Leesburg, FL

Everyone loves this soft peanut brittle and it's easier to eat than regular peanut brittle. The secret is quick cooling!

2 c. creamy peanut butter
1-1/2 c. sugar
1-1/2 c. light corn syrup
1/4 c. plus 2 t. water, divided

2 T. butter
2 c. raw or roasted peanuts
1 t. baking soda
1 t. vanilla extract

In a double boiler over hot water, place peanut butter to warm while preparing syrup. In a large saucepan, combine sugar, corn syrup and 1/4 cup water. Cook over high heat until mixture reaches the soft-crack stage, or 275 degrees on a candy thermometer. Reduce heat to medium; add butter and stir until melted. Add peanuts. Cook and stir for about 5 minutes, until candy starts to turn brown and reaches the hard-crack stage, or 300 degrees on thermometer. Remove from heat. Dissolve baking soda in remaining water; stir into mixture. Add vanilla. Working quickly, fold in warm peanut butter, stirring gently. All at once, pour candy mixture onto a greased marble slab or baking sheet. Quickly spread as thinly as possible. When cold, break into serving-size portions. Makes 3 pounds.

Maple Cream Candy

Tina Goodpasture
Meadowview, VA

I love this candy. It's simple to make, but has a big, sweet taste! Nuts may be added while beating, if desired.

1 c. pure maple syrup
1 c. sugar

1/2 c. whipping cream
1 T. butter

Combine all ingredients in a heavy saucepan. Cook over medium-low heat until sugar dissolves, stirring occasionally. Cook to soft-ball stage, or 234 to 243 degrees on a candy thermometer. Remove from heat; beat until cool and creamy. Pour into a buttered 8"x8" baking pan. Cool until set; cut into squares. Makes 2 dozen.

Delicious Down-Home Desserts

Spiced Sweet Potato Bundt Cake

Donna Wilson
Maryville, TN

This cake will make your home smell amazing, like fall. It always has the kids come around, asking, "What smells so good?"

3 eggs
2 c. sugar
1/2 c. applesauce
2 4-oz. jars strained sweet
   potato baby food

1 t. pumpkin pie spice
2 t. ground cloves
2 c. all-purpose flour
2 t. baking powder
Garnish: powdered sugar

Beat eggs in a large bowl. Add sugar, applesauce, baby food and spices; mix well. Add flour and baking powder; stir until well combined. Pour batter into a greased and floured Bundt® pan. Bake at 350 degrees for 50 minutes. Cool; turn out of pan onto a cake plate. Just before serving, sift powdered sugar over cake. Makes 12 servings.

For a little extra sweetness, drizzle a powdered sugar glaze over fresh-baked cakes, pies and cookies. Just add 2 tablespoons milk to 1-1/2 cups powdered sugar and stir until smooth.

Autumn Recipes from the Farmhouse

Caramel Fudge Cheesecake
Joyceann Dreibelbis
Wooster, OH

This dessert satisfies both the chocolate lover and the cheesecake lover with its fudgy crust, crunchy pecans and gooey layer of caramel. Plan ahead for the chilling time.

18.3-oz. pkg. fudge brownie mix
14-oz. pkg. caramels, unwrapped
1/4 c. evaporated milk
1-1/4 c. pecans, coarsely
   chopped
2 8-oz. pkgs. cream cheese,
   softened

1/2 c. sugar
2 eggs, beaten
2 1-oz. sqs. semi-sweet baking
   chocolate
2 1-oz. sqs. unsweetened baking
   chocolate

Prepare brownie batter according to the package. Spread batter in a greased 9" springform pan. Bake at 350 degrees for 20 minutes. Cool for 10 minutes on a wire rack. In a microwave-safe bowl, melt caramels with evaporated milk. Pour over brownie crust; sprinkle with pecans and set aside. In a bowl, combine cream cheese and sugar; beat well with an electric mixer on medium speed. Add eggs; beat on low speed just until combined. Melt chocolates in a small saucepan over very low heat, stirring constantly. Add melted chocolate to batter; pour over pecans. Bake at 350 degrees for 35 minutes, or until center is almost set. Cool on a wire rack for 10 minutes. Run a knife around edge of pan to loosen; cool completely. Cover and chill overnight. To serve, remove sides of pan; cut into wedges. Store any leftovers in the refrigerator. Makes 12 servings.

Mix up some mulling spice bags. Fill small muslin bags with one teaspoon each of whole cloves, allspice and orange zest plus 2 or 3 cinnamon sticks. Simmer in 2 quarts apple cider for a hot beverage that will warm you right up.

Delicious Down-Home Desserts

Betty's Lemon Pie

Allison Hayes
Jemison, AL

This recipe came from my grandmother, Betty. It's the easiest, most delicious treat! I hope you will enjoy this family recipe.

8-oz. pkg. cream cheese, softened
14-oz. can sweetened condensed milk

juice of 2 lemons
9-inch graham cracker pie crust

For best results, let cream cheese soften at room temperature for 3 hours. Combine cream cheese, condensed milk and lemon juice in a large bowl. Beat with an electric mixer on medium speed until mixture is smooth. Pour into crust. Cover and chill for 4 hours before serving. Cut into wedges. Makes 8 servings.

Company's Coming Cake

Judy Lange
Imperial, PA

Whenever company calls and says, "We're coming to visit!" we always used to whip this up. I hope you enjoy this cake as much as we do!

3.5-oz. pkg. cook & serve butterscotch pudding mix
2 c. milk

18-1/2 oz. pkg. yellow cake mix
11-oz. pkg. butterscotch chips
4-oz. pkg. chopped pecans

Prepare pudding with milk as directed on package; let cool. Mix pudding with dry cake mix. Pour batter into a greased 13"x9" baking pan. Sprinkle chips and nuts on top. Bake at 350 degrees for 35 to 40 minutes. Cut into squares. Makes 12 servings.

Write it on your heart that every day
is the best day of the year.
–Ralph Waldo Emerson

Autumn Recipes from the *Farmhouse*

Pineapple Sunshine Cake

Janet Rettig
Ward, AR

*A lady at church gave me this recipe more than
fifteen years ago. We really enjoy it.*

18-1/2 oz. pkg. yellow cake mix
4 eggs, beaten

1/2 c. oil
8-oz. can crushed pineapple

In a large bowl, combine dry cake mix, eggs, oil and pineapple with juice. Mix well. Pour batter into a 13"x9" baking pan coated with non-stick vegetable spray. Bake at 350 degrees for 25 to 30 minutes, until a toothpick inserted in the center comes out clean. Cool completely on a wire rack. Spread Frosting over cooled cake. Makes 12 servings.

Frosting:

8-oz. container frozen whipped
   topping, thawed
3.4-oz. pkg. instant vanilla
   pudding mix

8-oz. can crushed pineapple

In a bowl, fold together whipped topping, dry pudding mix and pineapple with juice.

Thanksgiving is a terrific time to catch up on the latest with everyone. Set up a memory table and ask everybody to bring along snapshots, clippings, even Junior's soccer trophy and Aunt Jane's latest knitting project...you'll all have so much to talk about!

Delicious Down-Home Desserts

Lemon-Glazed Pumpkin Cookies

Sandra Churchill
West Bridgewater, MA

On my wedding day, my Aunt Geri gave me the original version of this recipe. I have tweaked it, doubled the raisins, changed walnuts to pecans and changed the icing to a lemon glaze. It has become my family's favorite Thanksgiving tradition, after the turkey. My son and daughters even have a tradition of eating them while watching the Macy's Thanksgiving Day parade on Thanksgiving morning!

1/2 c. shortening
1 c. sugar
2 eggs, beaten
1 c. canned pumpkin
2 c. all-purpose flour
1 t. baking powder
1 t. salt

2-1/2 t. cinnamon
1/2 t. nutmeg
1/2 t. ground ginger
1-1/2 c. chopped pecans
1-1/2 c. raisins
1/2 c. sweetened dried
   cranberries

In a large bowl, blend together shortening and sugar. Add eggs and pumpkin; mix well. Add remaining ingredients; mix well. Drop dough by heaping tablespoonfuls onto greased baking sheets. Bake at 350 degrees for 15 to 18 minutes, until cookies are firm to the touch. Cool completely on wire racks, about one hour. Frost cookies with Icing and let dry. Makes 3 dozen.

Icing:

1 c. powdered sugar
3 T. lemon juice

1 t. lemon zest

Combine all ingredients; mix well to a spreadable consistency.

Younger guests will feel oh-so grown up when you serve them bubbly sparkling cider in long-stemmed plastic glasses.

Autumn Recipes
from the Farmhouse

Pride of Iowa Cookies

Vicki Van Donselaar
Cedar, IA

Being born, raised and living our entire life in Iowa, this is a fitting recipe for my husband and me. My grandma always had these cookies on hand when family members visited on Sunday afternoons. After I got married, I made these cookies for my husband while he was working in the field during harvest. He told me these cookies reminded him of a cookie his own grandma used to make. We wanted to share this recipe, since it brings back memories of both of our grandparents.

1 c. shortening
1 c. brown sugar, packed
1 c. sugar
2 eggs, beaten
2 c. all-purpose flour
1 t. baking powder
1 t. baking soda

1/2 t. salt
3 c. quick-cooking oats,
  uncooked
1 t. vanilla extract
1 c. chopped nuts
1 c. flaked coconut

In a large bowl, blend together shortening and sugars. Add eggs; beat well and set aside. In another bowl, sift together flour, baking powder, baking soda and salt. Add to shortening mixture; mix well. Stir in remaining ingredients. Roll dough into walnut-size balls. Place on baking sheets and press down with a fork. Bake at 350 degrees for about 9 minutes, until lightly golden. Makes about 3 dozen.

Whenever you bake favorite cookies and fruit breads, make a double batch to freeze. By the time the Christmas holidays arrive, you'll have a nice selection to share with guests...with no extra effort!

Delicious Down-Home Desserts

Carrot Cake Sandwich Cookies
Brenda Huey
Geneva, IN

These sandwich cookies taste just like a carrot cake! I make these in my bakery and they have been a favorite.

1 c. butter
1 c. brown sugar, packed
1 c. sugar
2 eggs, beaten
2 t. vanilla extract
2-1/2 c. all-purpose flour
1 c. rolled oats, uncooked

1 t. baking powder
1 t. baking soda
1/2 t. salt
1-1/2 t. cinnamon
1-1/3 c. carrots, peeled and
  grated
1/2 c. chopped pecans

In a large bowl, blend together butter, sugars, eggs and vanilla; set aside. In a separate bowl, mix flour, oats, baking powder, baking soda, salt and cinnamon. Slowly add flour mixture to butter mixture; stir just until combined. Stir in carrots and pecans. Drop dough in mounds by tablespoonfuls onto parchment paper-lined baking sheets, 2 inches apart. (Paper keeps cookies from spreading too much.) Bake at 350 degrees for 8 to 10 minutes, until set. Cool on baking sheets; and remove to a wire rack. Sandwich cookies together in pairs with Cream Cheese Icing. Makes 2 dozen.

Cream Cheese Icing:

1/2 c. butter
8-oz. pkg. cream cheese,
  softened

1 t. vanilla extract
4 c. powdered sugar

With an electric mixer on medium speed, beat butter, cream cheese and vanilla until creamy. Slowly beat in powdered sugar until well mixed.

Vintage napkins can often be found at tag sales...use them to wrap gifts from your kitchen or enjoy them on the dinner table!

Autumn Recipes from the Farmhouse

Maple-Cranberry Pudding Cake

Samantha Starks
Madison, WI

Mmm! Maple syrup and cranberries are two of our favorite autumn flavors. This recipe brings them together deliciously!

2 c. fresh or frozen cranberries
1 c. pure maple syrup
2/3 c. whipping cream
3/4 t. orange zest
2/3 c. all-purpose flour
1/3 c. cornmeal
1-1/2 t. baking powder
1/2 t. salt

1 egg, beaten
3 T. sugar
1/2 c. milk
1/2 c. butter, melted
1 t. vanilla extract
Garnish: whipped cream or
　vanilla ice cream

In a saucepan over medium heat, combine cranberries, maple syrup, cream and orange zest. Bring to a boil, stirring occasionally. Reduce heat to medium-low; simmer for one minute and remove from heat. In a bowl, whisk together flour, cornmeal, baking powder and salt; set aside. In a large bowl, whisk together egg and sugar. Add milk, melted butter and vanilla to egg mixture. Add flour mixture to egg mixture; whisk to blend. Pour warm cranberry mixture into a greased 8"x8" baking pan; pour batter over top. Bake at 400 degrees for about 28 minutes, until golden and bubbly at the edges. Cool for 15 minutes. Serve topped with whipped cream or vanilla ice cream. Serves 6 to 8.

Pick up a couple pints of cinnamon ice cream when it's available... perfect for adding that special touch to holiday desserts.

Delicious Down-Home Desserts

Grandpa Mel's Caramel Corn
Melissa Clemens
Mansfield, OH

We loved to hear Dad in the kitchen getting the popcorn popper heated up on the stove, because it usually meant we were having homemade caramel corn. He would pour the hot mixture into a huge metal roaster pan and set it out in the cold on our enclosed porch at the farm until it hardened. We couldn't wait until he brought it in, because it meant it was ready to eat...yum! Nuts can be added, but we usually enjoyed this treat plain. This can be made into popcorn balls, also.

8 c. popcorn, popped
2 c. light brown sugar, packed
1/2 c. original or mild molasses
1/2 c. light corn syrup
2 T. white vinegar
1 t. baking soda
1 T. butter

Place popcorn in a heatproof large bowl; remove any unpopped kernels and set aside. Combine brown sugar, molasses, corn syrup and vinegar in the top of a double boiler. Cook over medium heat, stirring constantly, until mixture reaches soft-boil stage, or 234 to 243 degrees on a candy thermometer. Remove from heat. Add baking soda and butter, stirring rapidly, until mixture becomes foamy, caramel-colored and very, very hot. Pour mixture over popcorn, stirring well to coat. Cool. Makes 12 servings.

A double boiler is a must for making candy or melting chocolate without scorching. To be sure the water in the bottom pan doesn't boil down too low, drop in a glass marble when you fill the pan. The marble will rattle when it's time to add more water.

Autumn Recipes from the Farmhouse

Candy Apples

Janis Parr
Ontario, Canada

These shiny red apples are a delicious old-fashioned treat that is good for you!

9 McIntosh apples
9 wooden treat sticks
1 c. boiling water

2 c. sugar
1/4 t. cream of tartar
few drops red food coloring

Rinse and dry apples; insert a wooden stick into the stem end of each apple and set aside. In the top of a double boiler, combine boiling water, sugar and cream of tartar. Bring slowly to a boil over medium heat, stirring constantly. Once boiling, do not stir while syrup changes to a yellow color; watch carefully. Remove from heat; stir in food coloring. Place top of double boiler with candy mixture into a pan of hot water during dipping. Dip apples, covering completely. Place on wax paper until set. Makes 9 apples.

Set little ones down with a bowl of fruit-flavored cereal rings and a piece of dental floss...they can make cereal necklaces (and nibble away!) while you're baking.

Delicious Down-Home Desserts

Apple Shortbread Crumble

Lori Ritchey
Denver, PA

I can never get enough fall recipes to try out and to share!
Take these yummy bars to a church function or school meeting,
or share them with friends over a pot of tea.

2 c. all-purpose flour	1/4 t. ground cloves
1/2 c. sugar	1/2 t. salt
1/2 t. baking powder	1 c. butter, softened
1/2 t. cinnamon	21-oz. can apple pie filling
1/4 t. nutmeg	Optional: vanilla ice cream

In a large bowl, combine flour, sugar, baking powder, spices and salt.
Using a pastry blender or 2 forks, cut butter into flour mixture until
coarse crumbs form. Reserve one cup crumb mixture; press remaining
mixture into the bottom of a greased 8"x8" baking pan. Top with pie
filling; sprinkle reserved crumb mixture over filling. Bake at 375 degrees
for 30 minutes, or until lightly golden. Serve warm with vanilla ice
cream, or cool and cut into bars. Makes 2 dozen.

Keep apple pie spice on hand to use in all kinds of desserts.
A blend of cinnamon, nutmeg and allspice, it's like a spice
rack in a bottle!

Autumn Recipes from the Farmhouse

Scarecrow Corn Flake Cookies

Lynda Hart
Bluffdale, UT

These easy no-bake cookies are great for fall parties.

1 c. sugar
1 c. light corn syrup
1 c. creamy or chunky peanut butter

6 c. corn flake cereal
1/2 c. semi-sweet chocolate chips
1 T. butter

Mix sugar and corn syrup in a large saucepan; bring to a boil. Boil for just one minute; remove from heat. Add peanut butter and mix well. Add corn flakes, stirring to coat all of the flakes. Drop by tablespoonfuls onto wax paper. In a small saucepan over low heat, melt chocolate chips with butter, stirring until smooth. Drop a small amount of chocolate mixture onto each cookie. Store in an airtight container; do not refrigerate. Makes 3 to 4 dozen.

Crispy Treat Fudge

Lynda Robson
Boston, MA

Chocolatey, crispy bars in a jiffy...yum!

1/4 c. butter
1/4 c. corn syrup
1 c. semi-sweet chocolate chips

1 t. vanilla extract
1/2 c. powdered sugar
2 c. crispy rice cereal

In a large saucepan over low heat, combine butter, corn syrup and chocolate chips. Cook, stirring constantly, until smooth. Stir in vanilla and powdered sugar, mixing until smooth. Add cereal, mixing well. Spread mixture in a lightly buttered 8"x8" baking pan. Cover and chill until set, about 30 minutes. Cut into bars. Store in refrigerator. Makes 1-1/2 dozen.

An easy party treat...top chocolate-frosted cupcakes with candy pumpkins and a sprinkle of green-tinted coconut "grass."

Delicious Down-Home Desserts

Mom's Pumpkin Spice Cut-Out Cookies

Patricia Addison
Cave Junction, OR

This is a simple sugar cookie recipe, with some pumpkin pie spice added to it to give an autumny flavor for Halloween. Mom used to cut out cookies in the shapes of black cats, ghosts, witches and pumpkins. She'd use some of the cookies to decorate a "haunted graveyard" cake. So much fun for Halloween parties!

1. c. shortening
2 c. sugar
2 eggs, beaten
1 c. sour cream
1 t. vanilla extract
4-1/2 c. all-purpose flour

4 t. baking powder
1/2 t. baking soda
1/2 t. salt
1 t. pumpkin pie spice
Garnish: assorted colored
    frostings

In a bowl, blend shortening and sugar together. Add eggs, sour cream and vanilla; mix well and set aside. In a separate large bowl, combine flour, baking powder, baking soda, salt and spice; mix well. Stir in shortening mixture. Cover and chill dough about one hour. On a floured surface, roll out dough 1/4-inch thick. Cut out desired shapes with cookie cutters. Arrange cookies on lightly greased or parchment paper-lined baking sheets. Bake at 350 degrees for 12 minutes. Cool for 2 to 3 minutes on the baking sheets; remove cookies to wire racks to finish cooling. Frost with Halloween colors of yellow, orange, red and black. Makes 2 to 4 dozen.

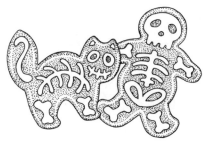

Mix up some frosting for Halloween cookies. For orange pumpkins, add 6 drops yellow and 2 drops red food coloring to a small bowl of white frosting. For black bats, cats and witches' hats, add 2 to 3 drops blue food coloring to a small bowl of dark chocolate frosting. Simple!

Banana Spice Cookies

Nanette Beane
Clarion, PA

I've had this recipe since I was in the seventh grade. It's a real keeper...great for after-school snacks!

1/2 c. shortening
1 c. brown sugar, packed
2 eggs, beaten
2 ripe bananas, mashed
2 c. all-purpose flour
2 t. baking powder

1/4 t. baking soda
1/4 t. salt
1/2 t. cinnamon
1/4 t. ground cloves
1/2 c. chopped nuts

In a large bowl, combine shortening, brown sugar, eggs and bananas; mix until smooth. Stir in remaining ingredients. Cover and chill for about one hour. Drop dough by rounded teaspoonfuls onto greased baking sheets, 2 inches apart. Bake at 375 degrees for 8 to 10 minutes. Cool cookies on wire racks; frost with Lemon Frosting. Makes 2 dozen.

Lemon Frosting:

1/3 c. butter, softened
3 c. powdered sugar

1 T. lemon juice
1/2 t. lemon zest

Combine all ingredients; stir until smooth.

After a farmhouse-size dinner, a simple dessert is perfect.
Enjoy assorted homemade cookies accompanied by scoops of
sherbet or fruit salad in footed dishes.

Delicious Down-Home Desserts

Chocolate-Walnut Sheet Cake

JoAnn
Gooseberry Patch

This great recipe makes enough servings for the whole hayride crowd.

1-1/4 c. butter, divided
1/2 c. baking cocoa, divided
1 c. water
2 c. all-purpose flour
1-1/2 c. brown sugar, packed
1 t. baking soda
1 t. cinnamon

1/2 t. salt
14-oz. can sweetened condensed
  milk, divided
2 eggs, beaten
1 t. vanilla extract
1 c. powdered sugar
1-1/2 c. chopped walnuts

Melt one cup butter in a saucepan over medium heat; stir in 1/4 cup cocoa and water. Bring to a boil; remove from heat. In a large bowl, combine flour, brown sugar, baking soda, cinnamon and salt. Add butter mixture, 1/3 cup condensed milk, eggs and vanilla. Beat with an electric mixer on medium speed until well mixed. Pour batter into a greased 15"x10" jelly-roll pan. Bake at 350 degrees for 15 minutes, or until top is firm to the touch. In another saucepan, melt remaining butter with remaining condensed milk and cocoa. Stir in powdered sugar until smooth; fold in walnuts. Spread frosting over warm cake. Makes 20 servings.

Scoops of ice cream are a perfect garnish for warm autumn pies, or alongside pieces of cake. Serve them in a snap...simply scoop ahead of time into paper muffin liners and freeze on a baking sheet.

Autumn Recipes from the Farmhouse

Pumpkin-Chocolate Chip Bars
Marsha Baker
Pioneer, OH

A lovely treat for anytime fall fun. Use white chocolate chips, if you like. Get ready to hear the oohs and aahs!

2 c. all-purpose flour
1 t. baking soda
1 t. pumpkin pie spice
   or cinnamon
1/4 t. salt
1 c. brown sugar, packed

1 c. butter, softened
1 c. canned pumpkin
1 egg, beaten
1 t. vanilla extract
1 c. semi-sweet chocolate chips,
   divided

In a bowl, whisk together flour, baking soda, spice and salt; set aside. In a large bowl, beat together brown sugar and butter. Blend in pumpkin, egg and vanilla; mix well. Add flour mixture and beat just until combined. Fold in 3/4 cup chocolate chips; pour batter into a greased 13"x9" baking pan. Spread batter evenly; sprinkle remaining chips over batter. Bake at 350 degrees for 30 to 35 minutes, until top springs back when touched. Cool; cut into bars. Makes one to 1-1/4 dozen.

Date-Nut Roll
Mary Coker
Apache Junction, AZ

My mother used to make this recipe. So easy and delicious...rich and wonderful! Very good served with a cup of coffee or tea.

25 graham crackers, crushed
4 c. chopped pecans
4 c. chopped dates

25 large marshmallows
1/2 c. milk
Optional: whipped cream

Mix graham cracker crumbs, pecans and dates in a large bowl; set aside. In the top of a double boiler over hot water, melt marshmallows in milk; add to crumb mixture and mix well. Spoon mixture onto wax paper and form into a long roll with your hands. Wrap and chill. To serve, slice in 1/4-inch slices. Top with whipped cream, if desired. Makes 12 servings.

Delicious Down-Home Desserts

Aleila's Raisin Cupcakes

Linda Basham
Gardner, IL

My grandma, Aleila Pfeifer, taught me to make these cupcakes when I was a child on the farm. We would have them for breakfast, or Grandma would have them ready for our tea parties after we got home from school. Tasty and very good for you!

1-1/2 c. raisins	1 egg, beaten
1-3/4 c. all-purpose flour, divided	1 t. baking soda
	1 t. nutmeg
1/4 c. butter, softened	1 t. cinnamon
3/4 c. sugar	1 c. chopped walnuts

Place raisins in a small saucepan; add enough water to cover. Bring to a boil over medium-high heat. Reduce heat to medium-low and simmer for 20 minutes. Drain, reserving 1/2 cup water. Place raisins in a bowl; add 1/4 cup flour and toss to coat well. (Flour will prevent raisins from sinking in the cupcakes.) In another bowl, blend butter and sugar. Add egg, baking soda, spices and raisins. Add chopped nuts and remaining flour; mix gently. Spoon batter into 12 paper-lined muffin cups, filling 2/3 full. Bake at 350 degrees for 20 minutes, or until a toothpick comes out clean. Set pan on a wire rack for 10 minutes; carefully remove to wire rack and cool completely. Makes one dozen.

With the holidays just around the corner, its' a good time to check your spice rack! Crush a pinch of each spice. If it has a fresh, zingy scent, it's still good. Toss out old–smelling spices and stock up on any that you've used up during the year.

INDEX

Appetizers & Snacks

Beverages

Breads

Breakfasts

INDEX

INDEX

Find Gooseberry Patch
wherever you are!

www.gooseberrypatch.com

Call us toll-free at 1·800·854·6673

homecoming parades · colorful leaves

drives in the country

craft fairs

casual get-togethers

moonlit hayrides

crackling bonfires · community suppers

U.S. to Metric Recipe Equivalents

Volume Measurements

1/4 teaspoon	1 mL
1/2 teaspoon	2 mL
1 teaspoon	5 mL
1 tablespoon = 3 teaspoons	15 mL
2 tablespoons = 1 fluid ounce	30 mL
1/4 cup	60 mL
1/3 cup	75 mL
1/2 cup = 4 fluid ounces	125 mL
1 cup = 8 fluid ounces	250 mL
2 cups = 1 pint =16 fluid ounces	500 mL
4 cups = 1 quart	1 L

Weights

1 ounce	30 g
4 ounces	120 g
8 ounces	225 g
16 ounces = 1 pound	450 g

Oven Temperatures

300° F	150° C
325° F	160° C
350° F	180° C
375° F	190° C
400° F	200° C
450° F	230° C

Baking Pan Sizes

Square		Loaf	
8x8x2 inches	2 L = 20x20x5 cm	9x5x3 inches	2 L = 23x13x7 cm
9x9x2 inches	2.5 L = 23x23x5 cm	Round	
Rectangular		8x1-1/2 inches	1.2 L = 20x4 cm
13x9x2 inches	3.5 L = 33x23x5 cm	9x1-1/2 inches	1.5 L = 23x4 cm